Food and Architecture

Food and Architecture

Prof. (Chef) Subhadip Majumder and
Ar. Sounak Majumder

BEP

BUSINESS EXPERT PRESS

Leader in applied, concise business books

Food and Architecture

Cover image licensed by Ingram Image, StockPhotoSecrets.com

Cover and interior design by Exeter Premedia Services Private Ltd., Chennai, India

First published in 2020 by
Business Expert Press, LLC
222 East 46th Street, New York, NY 10017
www.businessexpertpress.com

ISBN-13: 978-1-95253-848-3 (paperback)
ISBN-13: 978-1-95253-849-0 (e-book)

Business Expert Press Tourism and Hospitality Management Collection

Collection ISSN: 2375-9623 (print)
Collection ISSN: 2375-9631 (electronic)

First edition: 2020

10 9 8 7 6 5 4 3 2 1

Printed in the United States of America.

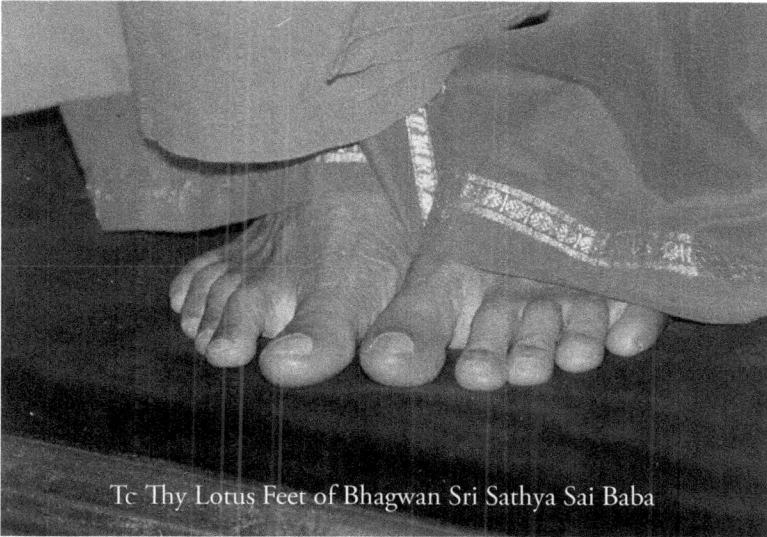

To Thy Lotus Feet of Bhagwan Sri Sathya Sai Baba

This book is a humble tribute to
Late Ms. Sulagna (Majumder) Dey
Late Mr. Dhiraj Dey
Late Mr. Subhamoy Majumder
We would like to thank our entire family members, respected teachers, friends and juniors whose constant support has really helped us to finish the book with an extremely positive mind frame.

Abstract

Food and architecture, the two pillars of human civilisation have inter-twined to such extents to sustain the civilization itself that the connection between the two has visually ceased to exist. The apparent diverse fields of human life have worked upon similar principles through ages from the beginning of mankind and they complemented our existence.

Eating is an activity that appeals to all our senses daily. Food is fundamental to cross-cultural studies of behaviour, thought, and imagery. We eat for many reasons than just to satisfy our stomach. Also, there is a factor that relates to our connection of food and society. Be it with family or friends, the act of eating is now a way of socializing with others. The food is the common focal point for the host and the visitor. It supplies the vast majority of dramatization, energy, and communication and it tumbles to the chef to create food that is tasty and alluring. And major institutes of food service that deals regularly with hundreds of publics try to thrive their users with a built environment keeping the food as the main focal point. Although most of the users might not understand the thought consciously but subconscious mind keeps alarming when things don't fall in place.

Taking this to the next level comes the process part of these diverse fields. Breaking down each process to a simpler logic would give us a similar flow that is strikingly astonishing. And from the micro level of food presentation to the macro level of food production, even on the farmlands, the process complements or get complemented through the immediate built-scape.

The book surfs through all the aspects of such two diverse fields and tries to show a parallel through a very socialistic and holistic perspective. It's interesting to understand the intangible logics behind the very tangible aspects of human life.

Contents

Contents

Acknowledgment

Although only our names appear on the cover of this book, a great many people have contributed for its completion. We owe our gratitude to all those people who have made this research for this book possible and because of whom our journey as authors and largely as human beings has been so enjoyable.

Our deepest gratitude to Chef Manjit Singh Gill (Corporate Chef, ITC group), Chef Saby (Lavaash), Mr. Mayank Taneja (Mish Horesha) and Dr. Amit Hajela (Urban Designer, Neev Architects) who cooperated with us and helped us through all possible means and imparted priceless knowledge without which the book could have never become a reality.

We are also indebted to Mr. Madan S. Rajan and Ar. Vinti Agarwal for showing such patience and editing and compiling repeatedly and bearing with us in their busy schedule.

Most importantly, none of this would have been possible without the love and patience of our family. We would like to dedicate this work to Chef Subhamoy Majumder (father to Ar. Sounak and brother to Chef Subhadip), whom we lost physically few years back. May your omnipresent soul forever guide us in the right path.

Thank you very much everyone.

CHAPTER 1

Foreword

In my long teaching career, I have come across many such books available in bookshelves, but this document is surely of great support for those who really want to install their dream into reality in the world of hospitality.

I convey my deepest wish to Chef Subhadip and Architect Sounak for giving birth to such a unique creation and handing it over to the large community of budding culinary artists before they put in their strong and sustainable steps in this field and smell success in life.

God is great.

Chef Bonophool Banerjee
Senior Lecturer
IHM, Kolkata

Food and Architecture is a pop eye-opener for those who are still in search of dimensions of hospitality to improve their knowledge bank. Chef Subhadip is known to me for years and the kind of work he has delivered toward hospitality is something to be honoured but cannot be measured. At the same time Sounak who is an upcoming architect in the field of hospitality has shown devotion and passion toward this noble profession which surely would become an asset for a library to collect.

I wish both of them my deepest wishes on their road to success.

Mr. G. Raghubalan
Hospitality Trainer, Author

CHAPTER 2

Introduction to Food and Architecture

Food and architecture have always been two basic needs of human civilization. Though both these disciplines have been subconsciously practiced, consciously studied, and always innovated to achieve perfection for ages, the relation between them has not been seriously discussed except a mention in a few articles or journals. One of the reasons for this perhaps could be the huge number of similarities that these fields share in common.

Since time immemorial, mankind has developed over the years from being hunter-gatherers to peasants to a global industrial community producing a diverse range of products and services. But the driving force for this magnificent journey has always been food. The evolution from struggling for survival to the packaging and consumption of the finest culinary delicacies for the most luxurious dining experience has been a long and illuminating journey, and architecture too has always developed side by side. Be it the prehistoric settlements of Skara Brae or F. L. Wright's "FallingWater," the hearth has always taken the utmost importance in architectural design and been the focus around which the space has been conceived and designed.

These similarities can further be classified on the basis of "need–process–outcome," which are primary needs for mankind's survival. This surprisingly intricate process may look simple but it shapes expected outcomes and leads to the fulfillment of our desires.

Need

Food and architecture from early times have continually addressed our survival and sustainability. Whilst food gives us the energy to survive and thrive, architecture or the built-up environment around us protects us from hostile environments and helps us sustain ourselves for longer periods. Architecture also provides us with the capacity to store food, thereby ensuring our long-term survival. In modern times, beyond the paramount basic necessity of food and architecture, both (quite often together) fulfill our need to feel happy, refreshed, and enthusiastic.

Process

Food preparation and architectural designing both follow the simple basic rules of catering to function and visual aesthetics at the same time. The basic food ingredients for a chef correlate to basic building elements such as arches, columns, vaults, and domes for the architect. The process followed always aims toward a balanced and perfect combination of the raw ingredients within given constraints and is greatly or slightly modulated according to the taste of the user. Context plays a vital role while defining the process and is the single element that connects all other important factors.

Culture—The culture of every human society marks the needs and constraints of its individual members and hence warrants the utmost importance while performing the process. Today's society and culture are intertwined between political, economic, historical, and social features and this is Aptly reflected in its food and architecture.

Climate—While, in architecture, climate plays a decisive role in the overall form of architecture to tackle the harsh challenges of wind and weather, in gastronomy climate regulates the quality and quantity of production.

Economics—Economics plays a crucial part in shaping the minds of both chef and architect. It determines the raw materials to be used, the quality and quantity to be achieved, and the clientele to be served. A good chef or an architect is one who understands the overall economics and designs accordingly, while a still better one tries to merge the differences through the process and comes up with an outcome that becomes his or her individual signature among others.

Topography—It connects us with nature and helps us lay the foundation of the production process, thereby helping one to judge the path to be followed in form and function. Both food and built-up spaces can be adequately envisioned only if the topography is properly analyzed.

Outcome

While the process takes hours, days, or even months in both the cases, the user can only judge it through the outcome. Usually, architectural outcomes continue for years, but food experiences in comparison are rather temporal, as it takes only minutes to enjoy the product. But this isn't always true as nostalgia too plays a great role in the process. Remember the soup your uncle made? Or the chicken your father once prepared? At times, these experiences through food remain for a lifetime.

Language versus Cuisine—The first thing to be considered while appreciating any architectural work is its language and structure, which in terms of gastronomy can be related to varied cuisine. Knowledge of these particular features helps the user take informed decisions on the functional and aesthetic values of the product they are going to experience. Even if the cuisine or language is new to them, their experience sets a benchmark for the future.

Materiality versus Ingredients—Both in their respective fields solidify the concepts of the creator as they give the creation a physical appearance. Materiality largely defines the language and adds color, texture, flavor and essence that help in creating the aura. This can also govern economic factors to a great extent and is hence given the utmost importance by both the creator and the user.

Aesthetics versus Presentation—This factor in both fields helps in generating curiosity and eventually a sense of awe (if done successfully) in the user, thus producing a quick initial reaction in the subconscious mind of the user. Unimaginative presentation often fails to communicate the virtues of a certain creation and, as a result, the work loses its value in the eyes of the user.

Experience versus Taste—This is the last but most important character of any architectural or gastronomic intervention. The user in both cases pays for the taste or experience, which acts as the most dominant character, and this characteristic is formulated through combining all the other mentioned aspects. Hence, often through professional training or through inherent individual talent, the chef and the architectural designer learn the art of imagining the final outcome long before the process is performed.

CHAPTER 3

Food as an Experience

We are witnessing a time where dining is moving toward a formative and dynamic experience. Today, meals have become social events thereby transforming the dinner table into a major domain particularly in cities.

> Cities are home to over fifty percent of the world's population, a figure which is expected to increase enormously by 2050. Despite the growing demand on urban resources and infrastructure, food is still often overlooked as a key factor in planning and designing cities. Without incorporating food into the design process—how it is grown, transported, and bought, cooked, eaten, and disposed of, it is impossible to create truly resilient and convivial urbanism. (Parham 2015)

Eating Spaces in the Contemporary Era

We have entered a new era, a moment in architecture, where due to the pace of life and technology, cultures are continuously delocalized and are coming together to unfold new layers of modernism. This enriching influence is increasing the mix and broadening the current range existing in architecture. In case of evocative forms, of materials and colours, of social thinking and of cultural references, we are no longer constrained to local thought processes. After the age of boredom with its monocultures and orthodoxies, we are almost universally expecting that the metro-culture, be it in London, New York, Beijing, or Delhi, will provide us with an extended cultural experience in cuisine, fashion, art, and performance. The modern city with cultural and ethnical diversities is a place for stimulating encounters between traditions, ethnicities, and cultures; a place of daily contradictions, mixed signals, and delightful confusions:

Indo-Chinese cuisine, Anglo-Indian culture, Afro-American lifestyle—no matter what one's genetic culture, we are all becoming habituated to diverse rhythms and varied emotional accents. We are getting used to "alternative" ideas of beauty, and different schools of architecture are also incorporating these changes and trying to respond to them.

After the industrial revolution in the 18th century, cities have grown to be mega cities or so-called metropolises and have seen a lot of migration from backward areas mainly because of growing job opportunities and the global lifestyle offered by cities to their residents. This resulted in the creation of a cosmopolitan mix of cultures of various regions and the term metro-culture thus became hugely popular in the beginning of the 20th century with an increasing number of people aspiring to be a part of this process. But this trend also led to people leading a mechanical life, where humans were considered machines and a capitalist-consumerist lifestyle came in being. While everything is becoming standardized today, the very idea of "human" itself has become mechanized as we are ourselves becoming products.

Although modern-day restaurants by and large as a whole are a product of such capitalist ideas of city culture, lately these along with bars have become a social factor providing people with the much required respite in their mechanical lifestyles. With the rising popularity of thematic restaurants, people have started having a nostalgic relationship with these spaces even if those places were just a commercial replication of an idea—a hyper-reality created majorly by the capitalists to create a market which never existed.

> Our most intimate contact with nature occurs when we eat it.
> (Armrest 2003)

We, therefore, need to focus on the "gastronomic" possibilities of urban spaces which will result in the recreation and redefinition of sensitive architectural forms, details and so on, throughout the population. These two words can also facilitate the viewing of food and architecture in parallel lenses. In the field, professionals of both these disciplines keep on re-creating and redefining raw materials into products which often reach the pinnacle of being deemed as works of art!

The idea of preparing a meal and creating a place for having the meal is not isolated as the importance of food in any culture is identical to the concept of a kitchen in any habitat. The culture of any place, community or religion grows out of repetitive lifestyle experiences and hence food in any culture acts as a central factor as it is the most primitive need for all of the human race and for that matter all living beings. Hence, whenever any piece of architecture has been made to house a group of human beings, the hearth has been at its center as it is this space which caters to our most primitive needs. Work culture largely grew out of the need to supplement the hearth with resources and hence the kitchen which grew out of the hearth in a habitat became as important as the food in any culture.

CHAPTER 4

Contextualising Eating Spaces—A Study on Thematic Restaurants

Introduction

Brief History

The development of the first theme restaurants began in the later 19th century with the Paris cafés and cabarets which opened in Montmartre. They were mostly drinking spots, not proper restaurants, but they also served food. Like the thematic restaurants of recent days, they were built around a concept and created an atmosphere which appeared to be something more than an ordinary eating and drinking venue.

Figure 4.1 Cafe of hell

Source: Restaurantingthroughhistory.com

Figure 4.2 Café du Bagne

Source: Restaurantingthroughhistory.com

Initially these artistic cafes had a counter cultural motivation in many cases; for example, these cafes showcased the revolutionary Paris Commune of 1871, which was found to be deep-rooted in Montmartre. Maxime Lisbonne, who was a member of the commune and had been exiled to a South Pacific penal colony for a long time, started the Café du Bagne (Café of the Penitentiary) in 1885. It was one of the first among many such establishments. The café with its many practices addressed the commune heroes; the walls had posters imitating a prison eating hall and the waiters were dressed like convicts with balls and chains. Upon opening, the place became an instant success among the people and the community lined up outside for the experience. To fulfill his socialistic mission, Lisbonne announced a free breakfast for the poor residents of Montmartre, in 1886: "Come, and eat your fill, your appetite sharpened by the knowledge that it was from their [the capitalists] coffers the money was extracted."

The spirit of Pariss unconventional cafés passed on to the United States beginning with New York City. Initially these NY cafés were but a replication of some original French ones, but within a decade or so they started having their own original ideas as well.

Portrayal of a Different Time–Space

After the beginning of portraying political agendas, themes started varying from freezing a time, a particular tradition, a culture or a fairy tale, and with time these became as dynamic as a particular film or a person and started creating an almost heterotypic space which the customers were completely unaware of.

Recent Developments

Over the years, the spaces for dining have changed drastically. From the prehistoric hearth in the caves to the postmodern restaurants, bars, lounges and food-courts, spaces have evolved according to the specific needs of the human race.

Although restaurants and similar commercial eating-out spaces should have been the direct representation of the connection between food and architecture, this is not true in most cases. Keeping aside all the positivity of modernization, current urbanism has become over-dependent on standardization and hence all the restaurants in the city irrespective of what they are serving, be it Mexican, Chinese, Japanese, Italian or any Indian delicacy, tend to provide a similar architectural layout which eventually results in losing out the true essence of that particular cuisine; the authenticity of the cuisine doesn't only include the food that is being served; the way it is served to the place where it is served all play a decisive role and it is this overall experience that binds the customer and induces him to return again and again.

As the thematic restaurants became popular among the people of the city who were bored with the monotony of industrial life, a competition among the owners began to grow. A group of designers started thinking of completely new ideas on how to deliver to the people, while a major chunk of owners got inspired by the success of some already existing themes and tried to replicate these in their restaurants. This started a trend of copying, and copies of copies started flooding the market.

Designing the Theme

For a restaurant, success depends on providing diners with a unique eating experience and an elegant atmosphere that helps them relax and pay more attention to the details in space which will slowly reveal to them the inner aesthetics of the particular space. The creation of such an elegant atmosphere could enhance the connection between dining spaces and diners and also integrate their minds with the theme of space. To create such a space for guests to experience, the design materials need to be based on a restaurant's space, gastronomy, and economy and this demands a lot of expertise.

> *Theming is … a word for evocative design that is narrative and transports you to another time and place.*
>
> —Rockwell

The contemporary generation of today has become all about the other, "time and place" through Escapism.

> *Players [in reference to architects and designers] see powerful forces at work, particularly a growing public appetite for fantasy and escape from life's increasingly mundane reality.*
>
> —Russell 1997

The concept of escapism today is about being furnished with some other time, space, spot, climate, or surrounding environment that completely goes beyond the everyday experience of a person within any medium. In our present-day society, dining out can be observed as a very common phenomenon depicting escapism. More eateries are planning and changing their outlines to give some other space, time, spot, atmosphere, or environment for regular clients. In 1997, according to a statistics published by Michael Rubin of MRA International, "themed and theatrical dining represents one or two per cent of restaurants, and will go to maybe 10 per cent by early next century." Eating out has therefore become the quickest and cheapest means of escape to release the tensions of our day-to-day lives or as a way of entertainment for the people leading mundane stressful lifestyles.

> *The concept of escape itself has been an animal instinct, even a human tendency, since the beginnings of predator and prey. The concept of escape in the animal world requires the reaction to be of the physical type. This used to be true for humans; however, the concept of escape in our modern world has become more psychological.*
>
> —Simpson 2003

This can be illustrated by the following examples. Imagine a person in a Bengali-themed restaurant. The designer would look forward to present a Bengali context along with the meal. That may be the very distant sound of flowing water or an imagery of a boat flowing in the vast Ganges, moist climate, bamboo or mud detailing, clay crockery, sitting on the ground and so on, thereby creating an environment where the cuisine is best relished by the diner. Similarly, for an Italian restaurant, a contrast of ivory, chocolate, and warm walnut wood hues throughout the inner space would create an elegant atmosphere and give an illusion about the modern Milanese aesthetic concept.

> *As for the restaurant that specializes in Japanese cuisine, in addition to images of the four seasons, abundant vitality is more important to be presented.*
>
> —Gao 2012

The designers may also opt for a simple and shady space to visually contrast with the fresh seasonal elements. In the suspended dining area, a steadily rising path echoes the blooming cherry, suggesting the integral features of Japanese culture which pay more attention to nature.

> *Memory is mainly to serve the design and the expression of emotion but not as a direct means of expression. Diners in the dining room need to enjoy more natural and relaxing visual experience.*
>
> —Gao 2012

To signify nature and create a more soothing environment, designers nowadays try to avoid any material that invokes memories of industrialization and turn to applying plants, pools, brick, canvas, natural stones, and wood and other decorative materials available locally or from external places to create a warm and intimate dining environment. Here, diners will forget about their busy schedule and concentrate on seeing the chef working and thus enjoy the joys of creation right in front of them leading to the restaurant being a place that leaves diners with many cherished memories.

In the modern-day context, environment plays a key role in the complete enjoyment of a meal as the customers' liking for food and drinks varies enormously with a variation in these elements. A choice of atmosphere, menu and services within an establishment helps generate more business and this factor is always kept in mind whenever a restaurant having a specific theme is built, as it tries to capture the whole idea in a single plot, so that the customer is able to relate to the space.

> *The design of stand-alone restaurants should conform to the dominant existing or planned character of the surrounding neighbourhood. This can be accomplished through designs that feature interpretations of nearby building designs. Such features may include but are not limited to colour, forms, materials, proportional relationships and fenestration patterns.*
> —Restaurant Design Guidelines, The City of Scottsdale 2000

Context has always been crucial to any kind of building. Even the most avant-garde architecture needs to study the surrounding in detail before arriving at any form, but in case of restaurants the context may change depending on the cuisine being served. For a multi-cuisine restaurant though this may be difficult to achieve, but for a thematic one it is must because of the overall ambience the client is paying for.

As stated by Ada Louise Huxtable, more people

> *prefer to seek entertainment and escape from the disturbing or humdrum aspects of urban and suburban life.* With the apparent desire for amusement and experiences among the population, *"theme"*

and "entertainment" design have "become a dominant factor influencing design and real estate development decisions ... It is reshaping our expectations of what places can do for people."

—Beck 1999

People go to restaurants not only for food but also for entertainment, to surprise themselves to be out of their normal working environment and their residence. More and more, people pay attention to the source of the food and how it is made; therefore, restaurants will be great cuisines soon.

—Gao 2012

The author Gao, in his book *100 Restaurant Design Principles*, investigates different perspectives significant to the overall restaurant plan, including the eatery administration idea, foundation of brand picture, and association between various practical choices. He demonstrates that the mystery of an eatery's achievement lies in the special eating background it offers to its clients and it lets us know the stories about this creation process by the designers with various expert and social encounters.

The standards of restaurant designing are a broad idea, which exposes the guidelines and techniques over the course of eatery planning. The creators may quickly enhance their abilities to control the project, to analyze and to present it dynamically. The bird's-eye perspective of display rendering clearly demonstrates the internal space division and setting, under the direction of bolts perspectives of various regions which are straightforwardly conveyed to users to demonstrate the relationship between zones. The idea of a different layout, different detailing, different atmosphere, and different dining experience has been very prominently represented for various cuisines throughout the world, which the author signifies as the most important aspect behind their success stories.

Socially Produced Space

His is the difficult task of bridging the gap between the product and the work, and he is fated to live out the conflicts that arise as he desperately seeks to close the ever-widening gap between knowledge and creativity.

—Lefebvre 1992

But achieving this success becomes the toughest challenge for the designer or the architect. He occupies the most uncomfortable position for, as a scientist he is obliged to produce functional spaces within a specified framework and depend on repetition, whereas, while in search for inspiration, he has to play the role of an artist and someone sensitive to the user's needs.

Modern society's most intense and vibrant interaction takes place over tables and bars.

—Andreini 2000

Restaurants today are filled with innovative lighting, sitting arrangements, dramatic effects, and infinitely new surprise elements to make them a hot-spot, intimate venues or meeting places. They are designed to please the ever-changing mood of their fickle clientele and sometimes they are so dynamic that they can be termed as new every single day!

Continental cafes are "places to dwell-in." the kind of place you can spend your day in.

—Oldenburg 1999

As Oldenburg suggests in his book, a healthy way of life balances the three realms of a citizen's life: home life, the workplace and inclusively sociable places. Just like "rendezvous," in French culture, due to lack of any other English term, Oldenburg coins the term "third place," to describe the third and the most important realm of a modern citizen's life.

Oldenburg also suggests that the third place along with numerous other benefits brings out massive social value for the users and he further points out their historical importance as in the case of:

- The American tavern in the American Revolution
- The French café in the French Revolution
- The London coffee house during Enlightenment
- The Agora in Greek democracy

CONTEXTUALISING EATING SPACES   19

He indicates the suburban development and urban planning practices as the major causes behind the passing of such third places. He advocates the third place as a solution against the deterioration of the American society as it will redefine the individual approaches toward this interpersonal interaction.

And here, Lefebvre revisits the wide gap that separates the products of different professionals, like those of architects and planners, from their intended inhabitants, the users—citizens and individuals. The alienation of individuals from the built-up environment they will inhabit leads to a "disillusionment" that "leaves spaces empty—an emptiness only words can convey" (Lefebvre 1992).

The "Aura" of the Space

Walter Benjamin discusses the change in perception and its consequences with the advent of film and photography, in the 20th century, in his famous article "The Work of Art in the Age of Mechanical Reproduction." He describes the changes of "sense" within the entire human race. This perception of a visual work of art has changed radically and determinately and asks whether even a general perspective of human senses toward the work of art is legitimate enough.

> Even the most perfect reproduction of a work of art is lacking in one element: its presence in time and space, its unique existence at the place where it happens to be. This unique existence of the work of art determined the history to which it was subject throughout the time of its existence.
>
> —Benjamin 1936

And he continues to describe this lacking element as the "aura" of any particular work of art. Through the effects of urbanity and industrialization, particularly through the work of art, Benjamin tries to point out something definite about the contemporary era. He considers film and photography as major contributors toward this movement and addresses mechanical reproduction of art as the sole reason for the loss of aura. Since the aura represents the originality or the authenticity of the art, it cannot be duplicated. He further goes on to say that a painting ought to have an Aura of itself while the photograph may not as the photograph could be an image of an image but the painting retains its absolute originality.

Benjamin also focuses on the tension between the aura and the new modes of perception. The original work of art is losing its authority as the authority itself is eliminated and he agrees to the fact that the cameraman shows us a particular scene in a way a painting could never do. But, on the other hand, he describes painting as totalitarian as it directs the eye toward a specific thing, a specific object, place or a story, leaving other parts unfocused (sometimes even literally), in a manner to perceive the scene so that we are distracted from the art itself.

Upon reading Benjamin, the mind inquires as to what does it mean to place an aura on "someone" or "something?" Or is it even essential to reclaim the aura in the first place? Now anyone can go to a museum, a theater, a gallery, or a cinema and thus the mystical cult of the original has been broken. This new mode of art appreciation now therefore allows ways to new modes of distraction and deception.

For Benjamin though, the aura is dead and the object is consuming the man at the same time that man consumes it. The aesthetic interpretation of these reproducible objects lies in a temporal world where we truly don't participate. Not only our action but also our perceptions are directed toward what we don't feel. He agrees that for mass production the distance from the "aura" may be an easy option but losing it may have major political impacts which may or may not be beneficial for us.

> Yet Benjamin makes it clear that in this new age of mechanical reproduction the contemplation of a screen and the nature of the film itself has changed in such a way that the individual no longer contemplates the film per say; the film contemplates them.
>
> —Ginal 2008

We are increasingly submitting ourselves toward the reproduced images and this is not the cause but the symptoms of something terrible that is happening. All human beings are the victims of subjectivity in this era of mechanical reproduction. How do we now define the aesthetic representation of the work of art after the loss of the "aura?"

The mentality that consumerism and economic growth are cure-alls is one of the biggest obstacles to real sustainability, but any change seems impossible, unthinkable. Our contemporary paradox finds us relying for our wellbeing on consumer-driven economic growth that we actually can't afford—not in environmental, economic or social terms. Although architecture and design have long been seen as engines for consumerism and growth, increasing numbers of designers are concerned about the problems resulting from growth.

—Thorpe 2012

Creating the Image

Establishment of the restaurant's image not only needs the appropriate atmosphere to support but specially needs one or several decorative symbols to attract diners' attention and thus help them get a clear understanding about the whole space. In addition, the symbolic thematic element could also enhance the space's inner depth.

—Gao 2012

If a designer is to create a luxurious oriental dining space for targeted diners he may opt for several Chinese or oriental patterns as decorative elements to enrich the overall taste and image of the restaurant. There may be a combination of patterns that include number 8, goldfish, water, peony, scepter, bamboo, ancient coin, jade, and other Chinese traditional symbols which may not be mechanically replicated in space but by means of modern techniques applied on the painted walls and crystal chandeliers above, and this is exactly where the problem starts. With these symbols of a certain culture, we as designers start stereotyping the entire concept and deviate from its authenticity.

Indoor waterfalls, warm earth tones, whimsical tableware, oversized furniture, electric art objects—today's restaurants often look like modern-art museums rather than dining facilities, a fact that sometimes generates more comments about their décor than their menus.

—Schultz 2000

To create a certain experience, we sometimes tend to create a museum of certain cultures. But the food of any time, space, or culture cannot be enjoyed within a museum of objects where the person has no personal contact with the immediate surroundings.

Lefebvre indicates a similar problem: the problem of representations. Although architects cannot escape representations and tend to create an image internal to them, Lefebvre doubts the efficiency of the image in making the gap less between "Apparent expertise and the actually daily lived experience." He even argues that "the image kills," as the psychological connect between the well-read architect's images and the common inhabitant is never made.

Diners now expect an engaging and amusing atmosphere to add to the entire experience of dining, and more and more restaurant owners are trying to fulfill that craving with exciting, innovative designs. With the rising of the restaurant industry and its pre-eminence being put above overall entertainment, restaurant design is leading to more and more exciting approaches of dining. Therefore, anything that can improve the customers' perception of that food and to make him return is important and this is where the role of an architect comes into play: as the designer and the mood maker, he gives the restaurant its own identity and characterizes the surroundings of the restaurant with the image of the restaurant itself.

CHAPTER 5

Thematic Restaurants Round the Globe

Kommunalka Restaurant, Moscow

Figure 5.1 Kommunalka Restaurant, Moscow

Theme—The name Kommunalka means "communal apartment" – an apartment shared by two or more families of the kind that was widespread in the Soviet Union until the 1980s.

Origin of the Theme—Throughout the Soviet reign, there was a critical short supply of urban housing in comparison to the needs of the growing city population. The intensive urbanization and massive industrialization of the USSR in the 20th century added a huge burden on existing housing apartments.

But the Soviet Government began to prioritize sufficient housing only after the 1950s. During the 1917 revolution, 80 percent of the Russian population lived in rural villages and towns. By the 1990s, most of the same population was urbanized, resulting in high-density housing in the cities. In the Soviet Union, these city-housings were the government's property. It was distributed by governmental departments based on a standardized number of square metres per person and, as a rule, tenants had no choice over the housing they were offered.

In the cities of Russia, even till the 1970s, most families had to live in a single room, in communal apartments known as Kommunalka. This dramatic shift created new cultures and the restaurant tried to freeze the time of the 1970s in such an apartment when inhabitants suffered over crowdedness and had very little hope of improvement.

The Restaurant—Throughout the design, the notion of freezing time has been well depicted through different visual imageries. Since the flat itself has been constructed as a former communal apartment, it has the exact architectural features that were followed way back in the 1970s, so it can be assumed that the authenticity the owner is trying to sell has some original background. The architect has played with the existing décor of the place and mostly preserved in their pristine condition. Plenty of Soviet paraphernalia, including old television sets, radios, scales, and jars with pickles scattered around, takes you back visually to the preserved time. But due to the lack of information, it is not clear as to whether these elements are open to usage by customers or are just treated as elements for cultural appropriation, as usage of these elements while dining would be more successful in creating the environment in such a restaurant trying to sell the concept of freezing time, as all these neglected yet "authentic" elements carry the "aura" of the 1970s' soviet apartments which will be best experienced in their usage.

From the pictures of the space, it is clear that the space is trying to create a museum of a certain time frame. This has been the architect's contribution to bring out the Soviet essence of the space, which is certainly a great attempt in itself. But the fusion of the salad bar has huge internal conflicts with the theme and sometimes overpowers the Soviet aura. A more subtle introduction of the salad bar would have been much appreciated, although the crowded sitting layout portrays the crowded nature of such apartments, but is somehow a little too odd and shows commercialization of such a "homely space" too promptly. Rather a dining space with more flexibilities to the customer to decide his own space would have produced more interest in the diner's mind, and the playful nature of the space along with the physical interaction with the used objects would have helped the customers "live" in the past for a few hours, thereby creating a social space providing personal intervention which would have been the USP of the restaurant.

Nando's Restaurant, Adelaide, Australia

Figure 5.2 The Nando's Restaurant, Australia

Australian Farmyard Theme Design, Frame Magazine

The Australian farmyard theme reflects the aesthetic concept of returning to nature and draws inspiration from the Australian agriculture and countryside culture to improve the competitiveness of a restaurant and present the local characteristic and culture of the region.

In this case, the restaurant is located in a spacious Shopping Center which allows for the formation of a feature barn-like structure, inspired by the Australian countryside vernacular architecture. This fantastic area will effectively attract diners to come into the space and completely express the business philosophy that emphasizes healthy eating.

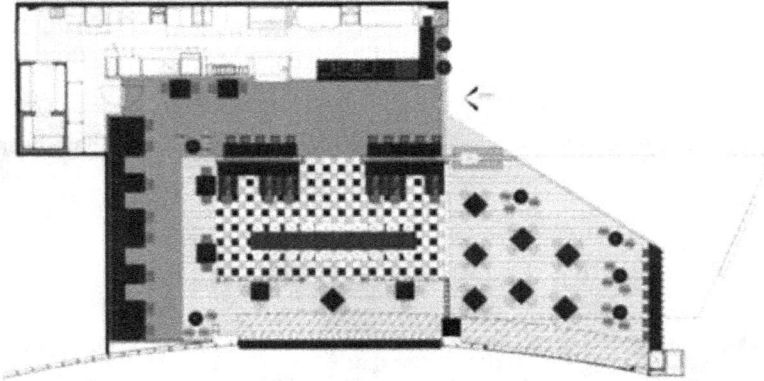

Figure 5.3 Plan of Nando's Restaurant, Australia

Source: 100 Restaurant Design Principles

- This restaurant concept was born out of the location, inspired by South Australia's rich agricultural and rural heritage.
- Rustic farmyard simplicity: an honest, raw, back-to-basics rural aesthetic.
- The generous volume allowed for the formation of a feature barn-like structure, inspired by the Australian countryside vernacular architecture.
- In essence, a simplified country shed—complete with exposed trusses, a raised, checked seating platform and coiled wire chicken-coop style pendants overhead.
- The perforated metal screening to the balustrades and kitchen wall insert hark back to the days of the rural Aussie meat safe.
- Timber farmyard fencing panels are suspended below the ceiling plane along the length of the space looking down into the mall below. The biggest challenge was considering the view from below as you look up into the space, and making full use of the volume to create a draw-card destination venue, enticing cinema-goers and diners up to the top floor of the Center.

Bukhara—Robust Flavours of the North-East Frontier

Theme—The theme of this restaurant revolves around the food it delivers, for which it takes the North-West Frontier of the colonized subcontinent. The North-West Frontier Province was demarcated in the year 1900, which today comprises parts of Afghanistan and the North-West part of pre-independent India. Bukhara delivers a cuisine that is deeply inspired from the traditions of these parts of the world, of enjoying a communal meal, "around the warm glow of a campfire—succulent tandoori fare, low on oil and high on authenticity" (ITC Hotels n.d.).

As per the corporate chef, Mr. Manjit Gill, the concept of the restaurant flows till the end of the meal and that's the factor that makes its customers wait for hours before actually getting inside the restaurant to have their meal.

Figure 5.4 Bukhara, ITC Maurya

Source: Author

Figure 5.5 Bukhara, ITC Maurya

Source: Author

Interior—The interior of the restaurant has been a product of thorough brainstorming by the designer, the owner, and the head chef. Hence, from the very beginning, all the interior elements have followed the same line of thoughts and a great balance between the use of visual imagery, crockery, flooring, seating, waiter's costumes, food, serving and its consumption has been successfully achieved. Elements such as hanging Bukhara carpets, suspended copper pots and urns along with stone wall and stone flooring like that of a very ordinary house of the region, earthenware crockery in an earthy ochre colour and menu painted on a block of wood inspire its customers to sit close to the floor with very low height stools, waiting for the food to come and chat in loud voices, just like they would in a bonfire and then enjoy the food with their companions. The absence of a spoon at the table inspires eating with hands and to accentuate this traditional effect, the servers are well trained to talk to the customer to be as friendly as they can to make sure the hands are used to enjoy the meal, as that's exactly what it takes to tear pieces of meat from the hard bones.

Figure 5.6 Details at Bukhara, ITC Maurya

Source: Author

Lavaash by Saby, Mehrauli, New Delhi

Figure 5.7 Lavaash, Mehrauli, Delhi

Source: www.lavaashbysaby.com

Theme—This restaurant represents the nostalgia of the celebrated chef and owner Sabyasachi Ghorai aka Chef Saby. The theme tells you a story of new culture reproduced out of the fusion of Armenians and Bengalis in the mining regions of Bengal, "coincidentally the place of my birth," says the chef. (Is it? Or in other words, representing our own culture is the most authentic way to do it in the first place!) The restaurant borrows its

name from the famous Armenian bread that has made its mark in UNE-
SCO's world heritage food, the first of its kind.

The Origin of the Theme; in Search of Authenticity—Chef Saby in his inter-
view beautifully depicts the story of how the theme came into place. It is
all rooted from his childhood memories and he gives his father the credit
behind the initial thought process. His father, professionally an anthro-
pologist and a known town planner, worked in the small twin towns
of Durgapur and Asansol. These places along with some similar towns
in eastern India contributed heavily to the industrial revolution due to
metallurgic advances brought in by the Armenians who were good at it.
As the two cultures met, a completely new style of Bengali–Armenian
cuisine evolved in these places which left an indelible mark in the food
culture of Bengal and the eastern regions.

As the theme stroked the chef's mind, he started researching this amal-
gamation. "I went to Armenian churches, talked to friends and families of
Armenian background, researched in the Webpages and came across a lot
of interesting facts; the menu and the interior, the food accessories to the
paintings, all depicts these amazing details."

Interestingly the famous tandoor was brought to India by these Armenian migrants in the name of Tonir and symbolized the Sun in the Armenian kitchen. It features as a major part in the menu as well, similar to
"Tolma" (which later became popular as 'Potoler Dolma' in Bengali cuisine) and Rogan josh (famous Indian meat curry with curd), in which the
paneer and curd themselves had an Armenian linkage.

Figure 5.8 Details at Lavaash, Mehrauli

Source: Author

Figure 5.9 Interior, Lavaash, Mehrauli

Source: Author

Interior—The interior of the restaurant is interesting and well laid out. The chef credits two young designers and Chef Megha Kohli in forming the initial mood boards leading to the final product. Chef Megha Kohli demonstrates that the elements used for the décor and for functional uses once had their origin in the then Bengal or Armenian households, and in certain cases the guests have been given the freedom to re-create the fusion that happened long ago.

The restaurant has a scratched clay texture on it, for which the designers have used "Ganges Ala mitti," which is predominantly a Bengali style to finish the kitchen walls due to its high smoke-absorbing capacity. Jute has been used abundantly throughout the space, be it the furniture, furnishings, eating accessories, or show pieces, as the first jute mills were set by Armenian traders in Calcutta (and now West Bengal is the highest jute producing state of the country). The craft of terracotta also had Armenian beginnings although the word terracotta later on became the image of Bengal and so did the fusion of Armenian embroidery and Bengali stitching, which we now know as the Katha stitch. Terracotta has been used for wall and floor tiling while Katha stitch has been a predominant element in all furnishings. Wooden furniture has been given preference to depict the old Armenian setting, unlike most restaurants that are now going in for steel or iron for their durability.

Figure 5.10 Bird motifs at Lavaash

Source: Author

The whole restaurant is decorated with hand-drawn bird motifs, where the peacock gets the maximum preference. Be it laser-cut ornamental partitions or handmade glass paintings to table tops, everything is linked to the abundance of birds in Armenian culture. But the presence of original birds in the veranda would have strengthened the concept. Also, the logo of Lavaash itself has taken the Armenian Bird calligraphy literally and represents each letter with peacocks. The use of brass metal and bell metal takes us to the time when steel was not introduced and their usage not only as lamp shades but also for cutlery makes an indelible mark in the user's mind. And these metal lamp shades are the only source of light during the night which is an appreciable attempt!

Figure 5.11 Lamps at Lavaash

Source: Author

Other Spaces—The restaurant is made within one of the oldest Sarais of Delhi. As per Chef Saby, "although this restaurant name was not there before industrial revolution, Sarai like this one have served travellers food for centuries." Hence the capitalist idea of a restaurant is just a layer of the overall idea of provision of food, a contribution of mechanized life and not the basic pillar of restaurants all over the world.

There are three spaces within the restaurant spread over two levels, a closed in-house setting with large arched windows allowing a lot of natural lights, a semi-covered veranda separated by a glass window with hand-painted Armenian motifs on it and a terrace.

The veranda has a lot of hand-painted motifs on the white wall and uses candles and yellow Edison bulbs which have a distant connection to a rural *zamindar*'s veranda, but may not be intentional. The terrace offers a grand view of the Qutub Minar and has a temporary setting which can be modulated.

Figure5.12 Veranda at Lavaash

Source: Author

Menu—The menu, in case of Lavaash, has been bonded to the theme and specifically offers those Armenian delicacies that were either a result of Bengali–Armenian cuisine or plucked from these two regions separately looking at the possibilities of complementing each other when served together. Each and every cocktail has a story to tell and some punches promote Bengal's local liquors with an urban touch, whilst others are inspired from the mining history of Asansol.

Figure 5.13 Delicacies at Lavaash

Source: Author

Madeleine's Madteater, Copenhagen

Figure 5.14 Madeleine's Madteater, Copenhagen

Recently, in the world of thematic dining experiences, Madeleine's Madteater (Mad—food, Teater—theater in Danish) has attracted widespread attention. It is a unique and unusual culinary experience combined with experimental theatrics. The theme automatically involves the diners and heightens their five senses thereby enhancing their experience with food.

The owners of Madeliene's Madteater—Mette Sia Martinussen and Nikolaj Danielsen—work together with well-known chefs, scientists, and musicians to bring this masterful dining experience into existence. The latest project, however, requires the diners to fast on the day of their visit. This is to encourage their physical and spiritual nourishment along with taste which, therefore, enhances the dining experience even further.

Figure 5.15 A gathering at Madeliene Madteater, Copenhagen

Today, dining out has become an urban dweller's chief form of recreation. Martinussen and Danielsen dream to keep on developing such food theaters to bridge the gap between the craving for superlative food and the related desire for more intangible qualities like meaning and community—qualities that a regular restaurant lack.

A restaurant that generates feelings like laughter, friendship, fear, shock, and joy is really something exceptional and a must visit for food enthusiasts all over the world.

Analysis

Personal Experience

Bukhara—No doubt Bukhara, being one of the oldest theme-based restaurants of the subcontinent, has been true to its authenticity and has humbly tried to replicate a particular cuisine and related habitual needs to enjoy the cuisine to its fullest. Bukhara being in a five-star hotel like ITC Maurya targets an audience which comes from a non-Indian background, and for them mostly being close to the earth, eating with their hands and taking the whole concept of eating out very informally is exotic. No "traditional music" and no "traditional essence" have been used which has added to the flavor, as doing that would have incorporated a fake North-East frontier idea which most restaurants with subcontinental themes do. The crisp selection of the menu clearly indicates that it inspired the overall design the most, and such restaurants have successfully stayed true to the framework of the menu for many long years. Though the space does look intimidating, it is also flexible enough to accommodate the varied psychological needs of different customers to a certain degree. Perhaps the visual imagery of suspended copper pots could have a functional value added to it but the flexibility of seating the diner directly on the ground could make this space more customer-centric and would have matched perfectly with the theme. But in the case of display kitchen, the permeation of the heat and the smell into the dining area would have been more intimidating and hence the display kitchen at a certain point resembles a fake or partial truth of something original.

Lavaash—This particular restaurant has the potential of being the social factor for all age groups. Although the first impression when someone enters the space is that of a common daily bar cum café, once the details are observed and the story behind them is heard, it will definitely make its mark. In spite of the restaurants own restrictions or rather limitations, somewhere the strong story behind the details are left unheard; reflect minute detail changes without making space for itself in the theme (like how the exterior areas don't use wooden furniture) or the completely unconnected English song playing in the background, but the total impact of the ambience, food, service, details, and the wonderful story of chef Saby should reach the ears of all Delhi dwellers in search for respite.

While cases like The Nando's make the mind enquire, what is it really like to live on a dairy farm in Australia? As traveller and blogger Mellisa from Canada describes:

> It's working on two shifts a day, its milking 650 cows, its feeding calves, it's napping in the middle of the day, it's being 1 hour away from a real town. It's a bit depressing. It's also challenging. You'll be able to save money as the farm will probably be out there, in a remote area. Surrounded by grass, hay and fields, you might be less stimulated. Your house will be surrounded by Australian locals; the kind of locals that bite, land on you and stick on your window.

Therefore, in order to critically analyze these restaurants, we need to ascertain whether these restaurants are focusing just on symbols of appropriation, or the architectural space is compelling the customer to re-create and reproduce the thematic experience.

So, a case like Nando's is really being problematic in the sense that they are achieving a beautiful product without understanding the psychological needs which in this case become the functional need as well, whilst places like Lavaash are helping you live a story and re-create some of it for yourself.

So, if this is the true essence of being in the space, is it being designed, consumed or even marketed in a way keeping in mind its true nature? Is the culture simply reproduced by the customers or is it just symbolized crudely to take the consumers into a hyper-real realm?

CHAPTER 6

Social Need of Thematic Restaurants

"I still think a place like Murthal will survive the industry much longer than any thematic one, it's still a need-based market," says Saby. So the question arises: are these spaces really required? Looking at the success story behind the case studies, it is clear that when a particular restaurant is feeding the market with something new, it is making a mark. It may create a hyper-real state but they are providing the city dweller the much needed third space as suggested by Oldenburg.

Understanding the Problem and a Step Toward Solution

Although these spaces seem to be popular, all of them are not, but why not? Because "90% of them are just into the cut-copy-paste mode where they are blindly taking objects from the rest 10% cases," as Chef Manjit Gill describes. Hence the reproduction has no meaning attached to it and the aura of the particular element as a visual imagery is getting lost and people at large are unable to associate themselves with it.

Cultural Appropriation

Taking intellectual property, traditional knowledge, cultural expressions, or artefacts from someone else's culture without permission can include unauthorized use of another culture's dance, dress, music, language, folklore, cuisine, traditional medicine, religious symbols, etc. It's most likely to be harmful when the source community is a minority group that has been oppressed or exploited in other ways or when the object of appropriation is particularly sensitive, for example, sacred objects. (Scafidi 2005)

It is quite common in the United States, where members of a dominant culture culturally appropriate a minority group by "borrowing" elements of that minority community. Afro-American natives, Asian Americans, and other indigenous cultures are generally targeted for such attention. Native American clothing, African dance and music, Asian cuisine, martial arts and dresses, all of these are victims of cultural appropriation.

So two questions arise:

- In case of a thematic restaurant does the person really pay loads of money for few symbols of a particular culture, or does he in his imagination try to live it in a given time frame?
- Second, even if we consider cultural appropriation ethically or morally viable, most of the restaurants in modern cities are unable to appropriate the culture to its fullest and rather simplify it to five to seven objects that may or may not have relevance in the original culture they are trying to showcase. How is this justified for the customer who is paying and the people whose culture is being exploited?

We need to understand here as to whether the "Stereotype" caused due to cultural appropriation is even helpful or not. Some themes such as that of the oriental one or majorly Chinese have been repeated so many times in restaurant history that it has made some original elements look stereotyped. The jade, goldfish, bamboo, and ancient coin might have had meaning to them initially and were original until mindless repetition took place. But there is another aspect to it and now after this mindless repetition, the image, howsoever fake it may be, has catered to the larger audience and hence they may not appreciate these repetitive elements, but their unconscious mind reacts to these elements much faster. So isn't that good? This reduces the hunger to know more and starts standardizing not only the elements but the themes themselves.

Ethics of Designing

Another major player in this context is ethical design. Ethics is a term, not for a code or a set of principles but for a discourse. In larger life, the architect has to answer these questions like for whose justice and rationality is he creating, whose ideologies are driving his intuitions and whether those ideologies are actually helpful for mankind in the larger perspective. But in the case of restaurant design, whatever type it may be, we must follow the restaurant ethics which boils down to the food delivered. "The new designers tend to design for their personal pleasure," says Chef Manjit Gill, and doesn't consider the chef's vision or the menu while designing.

"Ultimately it is a repeat business and the success lies on return of the customer multiple times," says Gill, and hence spaces where the theme overpowers may sustain the industry for a couple of years, but when the surprise element is gone it needs to find a way out. Nando's on one hand may surprise its customers with their barn structure, but it will surely fade away once people get nothing to re-create out of it. On the other hand, places like Lavaash or Bukhara will entangle your subconscious with the unique aura of the theme and consciously with the flavors of the food and will attract you for a much longer time. Hence in the case of creating a theme for the restaurant the combination of the owner, the chef, and the designer is a most ethical step toward conceptualization and each of them complements the expertise of others, and in that process even some stereotyped ideas may be redefined.

The Cartesian Problem and the Marxist Solution

Coming back to the question of the "Socially Produced Space" in Chapter 4, even if the space is appropriated, it should through its inhabitants help society turn spaces into places, an important vision so necessary to create social spaces.

Here, Marxism, specifically Marxist humanism, comes into play. It describes: *Man's essential nature is as a free producer, reproducing their own conditions of life.*

In capitalism, people are alienated from their productive activity and hence are compelled to sell their labor power. The idea of "geometrical space" can also be challenged as an idea of a space for an "empty area." Hence capitalism through Cartesian logic takes spaces as empty, and the social space or the social values of the space seem strange. All restaurant layouts have majorly restricted space to certain numerological values: 1.5 to

2.5 m² of area per person is what any restaurant design is all about. This idea in itself has made these spaces artificial, commercialized dead spaces which may decorate themselves with thousands of symbols but yet remain dead.

Lefebvre in his writings also describes the triad of spaces, the perceived, the conceived, and the lived. So when it comes to designing restaurants we need to keep in mind the perceived (used in everyday life) and the conceived (coded space of numbers by architects/planners) to create the lived space, a space that imagination seeks to create, to change, or to produce for itself.

We as architects need to focus on the material reconfiguration of the urban context in order to bring in a social reformation. Large-scale public consultation can surely be a way out, to listen to the grassroots' concerns. Like Benjamin described, "We as architects are always the bourgeois, the specialized producers, but we need to produce for the benefits of the proletariat, the commoners. Socialization needs to be an intrinsic unconscious process in our minds. We need to treat humans not as subjects but as users of the space."

Due to the failure of high modernist architecture, the views of socially and politically neutral architecture started being acknowledged. But space can never be neutral; rather it is the carrier and communicator of the ideologies that have contributed toward the shaping of it.

Authenticity

What is inauthentic living? It is the pressure to appear to be a certain kind of person, to adopt a particular kind of living, to ignore one's own moral and aesthetic value, and to have a more comfortable existence.

> *The existence of the original is prerequisite for authenticity*
> —Scafidi 2005

But again the authenticity and ethics of restaurant design pose difficulties while designing. Hence we must remember the customer's need and create something authentic out of it. There must be a fine balance between creation and ethics as we need to satisfy the capitalist layer, consciously putting it below the social layers and stopping standardization from happening as it will again bring a static nature to the space. So authenticity is not always about city-life comfort; rather it's more about the nature of a certain group of people in a certain place in a certain time which may or may not be pleasant, but yet can be an experience exotic enough to pay for.

The Process of Design

The process of design can never be linear and the problem starts at the point when it becomes such. The owner, the chef, and the designer are never individually working professionals when it comes to thematic designs but at the same time are parts of the whole and only then will the whole become greater than the sum of its parts. This process will have three stages:

1. Conceptualization
2. Implementation
3. Communication

The concept and the menu should be interconnected from the very beginning, just like the chef and the designer, as it is the food which should be the primary concern from an ethical perspective. Implementation will involve concreting the fluid concept into architectural elements and spaces. It should never compromise the conceptual needs of the project, and any restriction in the process should bring about conceptual changes and not be kept unaccounted for. The concept should evolve in a parallel fashion and not remain stagnant and these two stages will themselves produce factors for the third, "Communication," which will then translate the above two factors to the users of the space. It is also important that the three professionals of the team must remain unchanged and their minds unaffected by other thoughts. Any loose threads between these stages and these professionals may lead to a lack of complete realization of the concept within the design, and the resultant space might end up as just another among the thousands already prevalent in the market.

Restaurant Space Beyond Visual Imagery

We as architects must try to define space on the basis of its specificity and try to bridge the gap between the practical and theoretical realms, between mental and special, between people who deal with the space materialistically and the philosophers of the space. The world is full of inauthentic and highly politicized images. We need to reflect back onto ourselves after being absorbed by them.

This will only happen when the design transcends visual aesthetics and tries to disintegrate the mysteries of human existence itself in order to understand true human needs. The intellect, aesthetics, and the emotional part of the design process and the product must fuse into an embodied mental imagery which at the same time is diffused, compressed, metaphorical, and subconsciously permanent. The user of the thematic restaurant or the "user of the theme" should subconsciously react to the design during the 2 to 3 hours of stay, enjoy the meal and leave, leaving a part of himself in the space while also carrying a part of the space with himself. The theme must be an indivisible continuum of the external and the internal, the mental and the physical, the real and the imaginary.

The theme must be self-satisfactory, a universe in itself. The image must be powerful enough to present the intellectual and emotional complexities in an instant of time. Only such an idea can give us a sense of sudden liberation: the sense of freedom from space limits and time limits. As a designer we must acknowledge that it is not only the culture, time–space frame the theme is talking about, but also the chef and framework of the menu. These aspects should go parallel to each other from the very beginning of conceptualization. The team must be able to follow and correlate the three stages of designing.

Creating a Landmark

Although the restaurant in itself is one of the most capitalist institutions but from the designers point of view, in case it is a thematic one should consider it from a social point of view. As Foucault correctly analyzed that power and desire animate all participants at the micro level and not only in macro level such as state or corporations, any kind of built-up form will always have a capitalist "power-control" associated with it and that's true even for thematic spaces. But we, while creating a space for respite, must understand the space as a psychological need of the customer and provide numerous social layers to hide consumerist evil. We can't simply refuse power like most leftist ideologists, as it will continue to prevail, but we may create a more non-hegemonic space where such control is balanced and is not forced. Since the owner will always depend on economic profit out of the institution, it is justified to respect his needs but that shouldn't be the end of the design. It must be incorporated within and we must appreciate that success is not just making temporary money of a couple of years, but it is making a mark in society, in the cuisine industry. It's about creating a hunger for a specific feeling and about creating a restaurant as a landmark in itself.

CHAPTER 7

Food, Architecture, and Urbanism

Food is in architecture as architecture is in food—fashioned from raw materials into a cultural product. Hence the relationship between cooking, storing, serving, eating, and disposing operates as a food sphere, all contributing significantly toward the "production of space."

> *In 21st century, eating out has much to do with entertainment as with food. Restaurant owners, architects and designers nowadays create effective, themed and spectacular interiors, which are meant to seduce, impress and surprise us.*
>
> —Kunz and Fischer 2005

A fundamental change has been taking place in recent years in our urban public relationship with restaurants, bars, lounges, and so on. Higher expectations for everyday comforts, increased personal mobility, and the general desire to try out different experiences in the world of food have brought about many changes. As living has become more hectic, people have begun to view dining as one important form of nourishment and entertainment.

> *According to a recent survey, maximum percentage of people has eaten out in the last week, rather than any other form of activity.*
>
> —Das 2002

This trend has increased in the last few years, although eating out has been the source of entertainment for the human race for thousands of years. With so much interest and money riding on the food industry, it is extremely important for restaurant owners, designers, and architects to develop trends that positively impact customers for a much longer period of time. Restaurants are no more just places to eat, but have become a social factor in our day-to-day lives.

The food system has been gradually acknowledged to be a basic urban system for mankind, just like transportation and water supply systems. The interactions between these systems are becoming more evident and have been better understood today.

The food system reflects a rural system of flows, which are essentially managed by local, national and global agents through agricultural policies and expertise, to supply urban areas and fulfil their food needs through private entrepreneurs, with a little shaping by urban stakeholders. Access to food supply, through spaces such as markets, and the process of food production in the food industry have a significant impact on the built-up environment.

Today, however, it is the role of cities that are seen as fundamental to understanding and intervening in the food system. Also, the stability of the supply of food to urban areas and the adequate nourishment of citizens are becoming a growing cause for concern.

As a result, fields that work toward the design of urban settlements have begun to play a wide range of roles in shaping the urban food system as well, and they do so mainly by addressing their connections to the material settings where they normally work: home, their workplace, street, public space, and public institutions.

Food Urbanism

The production of food within and in close proximity to the urban milieu is termed as urban agriculture. This process is not restricted to a closed group of professionals in the primary sector, but is executed by a variety of agents including private individuals, groups or associations, public administrators, and professional farmers. The term urban farm refers to the general and spatial notion of a unit that produces food within the urban setting. The emerging practice of production of food within the urban context comes with a diverse range of scales and with different constraints than those observed in the rural context. For example, the food production that is considered to be at a large scale in an urban setting may correspond to small or medium scales of its rural counterpart. The process is executed by a variety of agents including private individuals, groups or associations, public administrators, and professional farmers.

There is no certain specific place for urban agriculture. All it needs is an idea, although few places can be commonly identified such as areas around collective dwellings, public transport stops, individual balconies, boulevards, urban squares, railroad wastelands, industrial wastelands, urban squares, public parks, and gardens. But the list is growing on a regular basis and with the emergence of green building practices, plants can be grown in almost any number of surfaces, be they horizontal, vertical, or any peculiar angle.

In the last few decades, the consciousness over food in the urban realm has led designers to focus on "food quarters," while designing an urban locality.

Now, what is a food quarter?

A 'fuzzy-edged' food centered area of an urban settlement, predicated on human scale, highly mixed, walkable and finely grained.
—Hall and Gössling 2016

Food quarters are a necessary replacement of the urban markets of the 20th century. They encompass all aspects of the gastronomy industry which traditional markets or even the farmers market failed to deliver. They support a varied range of food-related activities and land use. Generally grown around a central vegetable market, they incorporate restaurants, street food areas, small-scale production units, and so on, while supporting various consumption techniques including online marketing. Hence modern urban designers need to focus on such spaces as a module that can be developed and also retrofitted in various urban contexts and these can be the hotspot for medium-scale urban agriculture, where the community can participate. These spaces can further develop into small hubs in the locality, not only for their functional and recreational needs, but also as a community space for gathering, learning, and spreading awareness.

CHAPTER 8

Food Park: Developing a Sustainable Module

In 2050, the world population will rise to 9 billion people, an increase of 2 billion over 2018. Increasing prosperity in emerging countries automatically means a growing demand for qualitatively better food. If we want to ensure food security sustainably, we must make more efficient use of raw materials and energy while reducing food waste. At present, 25 to 30 percent of food products are wasted somewhere in the chain or are used for low-value applications.

India has been experiencing a high rate of economic growth in the last two decades but this growth has been contrasted with a high rate of food price inflation. The growth has been very uneven across sectors with agriculture in particular remaining very sluggish. The increase in per capita income has significantly increased the demand for food but agricultural production has failed to keep pace with the growing demand which is the major cause for price inflation.

India has always been blessed with huge agricultural potential. The huge plain land masses, with numerous major rivers flowing through them, have made a large part of India exceptionally fertile. This feature, throughout history, has helped most of the population to have at least the minimum food required to sustain itself. Also, throughout time our ancestors and ancient manuscripts have hailed food, prayed to the farmlands and the produce. Hence the whole process of production, consumption, and re-utilization of unused produce always had a social value attached to it.

But with industrialization the whole concept of eating changed largely from the hearth of the home to the numerous restaurants, eating joints, and quick food outlets. Food itself became the commodity. With globalization, various kinds of cuisine became available and the demand for imported food also increased. Hence large corporations saw this as a great capitalist opportunity for selling food products and its processes. Huge demand was generated and packaging, marketing, and branding became hugely important. Somewhere in all this, the sustainable values that we had persevered with for years got lost along the wayside. The middleman became the most important cog in the food chain and farmers began losing their rightful share of market. As a result, although 50 percent of the country's population is still in agricultural or allied facilities, agriculture contributes to only 15 percent of the GDP.

Hence, the need of the hour is a solution that reduces wastage, increases public awareness about food-related processes, and celebrates edible products not only as an important energy resource or for the mesmerizing taste they impart, but also as an important sector of India's blooming economy. We need to understand how major elements of the food industry can be intertwined into a larger framework to develop a sustainable food chain in the city, which in future could be replicated in different parts of the country, for an urban scale sustainability in the sector.

The Growing Need of Food Parks in India

India is called the fruit and vegetable basket of the world. The second largest producer next to China, its potential for being the largest food exporter in the world reflects not only in the quantity but also in the large variety of food available in the country. Among all the produced foods, hardly 2 percent is processed; due to lack of processing facilities there is a wastage of about 35 percent of the agricultural produce worth about US$10 billion. It is in this backdrop that food parks have become a necessity to provide the crucial link between the farmers and traders. Studies have shown that the food processing industry has an untapped domestic market of 1 billion consumers in the country, and hence has been accorded the status of priority sector in the new trade policy of the government. There is a huge potential in food processing industry for further development of India and food parks create a synergy between the two pillars of the economy—industry and agriculture.

Due to the decentralized systems of food processing, cooking, and disposing, various agencies like the Indian airways, hospitals, QSRs, and banquets are unable to run their present business model efficiently and in the most cost-optimal manner. The overall costing for buying raw materials, storage, staff maintenance, garbage disposal and recycling, and so on becomes much higher for all individual players. Also, very less or no energy is regained in any of the production units as their size makes them economically nonviable.

Field experts, though, are seeing potential in a much larger kitchen area that would serve all buildings in a given proximity. This along with reduction in space requirements and costing also makes the best use of all sustainable practices from reusing, reducing, and recycling to energy generation and completely organic in-house vegetation. Although the Ministry of Food Industries has proposed several food parks across the country, the crucial component of human interaction has been totally ignored. The possibilities of involving common people into the overall process of food and allied industry need to be explored.

Additionally, research and development in this growing sector needs to be handled more professionally. According to the industry experts, there is a severe lack of food-related research centers throughout the country, where professionals, young entrepreneurs, producers, and end-users can come together and do specific scientific researches on specific products and discuss the alternatives, pros, and cons logically.

The innovations that are taking place in the industry don't reach the common people as they don't get enough opportunities to be included. It has been surveyed that 85 percent of the self-help groups that work for food and allied activities don't have access to proper hygienic conditions, proper equipment, knowledge of cost-effective and sustainable practices, proper marketing strategies, and so on. Hence, the products made by the groups cannot earn enough margin and are not able to reach larger sections of the society. Due to these difficulties, a common facility to enhance the growing sector of food and allied activities is the need of the hour. Going with the new generation, food is no longer just a commodity for survival, but has, today, become a style statement. Hence, its process, products, and players need to be celebrated, so that along with strongly supporting the Indian and individual economy, it also becomes the source of knowledge and entertainment.

CHAPTER 9

Food Park: Designing the Module at Samalkha, Delhi

Conceptualization

Capitalizing the legacy of a food-imbibed culture of Delhi, the module, at a close proximity to major food and transit hubs, intends to become the wining, dining, and recreational destination of the city, offering a democratic inclusive space for interaction, socialization, congregation, and celebration of the notion of food in itself.

A multi-utility food park, along with catering to functional needs, will also cater to the city's food fantasies, aim at becoming a large catchment area for people around the city and also attract global attention of becoming a one-of-its-kind complex weaving together various food-related components.

Designing a complex to celebrate food and allied activities starting from production, processing, manufacturing, packaging, preparation, presentation till the disposal and recycling, the designed complex will aim at providing edutainment to visitors through its food and allied services; glorify techniques, technologies, skills, and latest developments; and also focus on minimizing area, cost, and energy requirements. What we need is an inspirational module so that it could be replicated in other parts of the city and become an efficient typology for the present urban structure.

Since the "food park" is a new typology of urban architectural prototypes, a suitable program needs to be developed to cater to the deficiencies of the existing systems and to create a commercially, socially, culturally, and environmentally viable project. The nature of the project is fairly complicated with the huge number of stakeholders to cater to. Hence equilibrium and a binding factor are required to help all the elements work individually, as well as remain strongly connected to each other. Since most of the elements of the complex are processes driven, cracking the schematic programs in coherence with other functions and the site is of utmost importance. While public areas like restaurants, stores, malls, and other exhibition spaces need to be active throughout the day, the agricultural and production part needs to be absolutely functional day and night.

The positive impact of different restrictions such as height restrictions and the presence of major food hubs in close proximity (detailed later on) should be taken into consideration in creating a larger food block throughout the locality. Also, the project must work as a module to be intelligently and efficiently replicated in various parts of the country for urban-level food sustainability.

Brief Study on Different Components of the Module

Food Court—Following the DLF Cyber Hub model, the food court in the project plays a major role as the main commercial component. It consists of each and every kind of restaurant and eatery, to satisfy every mood of the users. This majorly becomes the catchment of the public interface and hence also supports other functions in creating their individual markets (refer DLF Cyber Hub).

Research and Training Center—This is the educational facade of the project. With the mushrooming of thousands of hotel management and culinary institutes all over Delhi and NCR, the need to provide proper laboratory space and industrial-level training has become crucial. In-house employees also need periodic skill development programs that could be provided in-house from renowned chefs across the globe. A part of this component also exhibits the latest technological advancements in the field and provides leasable spaces for culinary programs such as Master Chef and Khana-Khazana and also to self-help groups that might use the in-house equipment on rent and are also given an opportunity to sell their products on-site (refer CFT, Allahabad University, Hotel Management Department, LPU).

Agro-Based Mall—Such malls were a previous initiative of the Haryana Government but the business model failed due to inaccessibility, as most of these malls were built along the agricultural belt which is far from any city. This also aims at providing a one-step solution for all food items, raw, packed, or processed, so that users can buy all world cuisine from a single place (refer proposed project for Punjab State Government, Neev Architects).

Main Kitchen—This is the industrial component of the scheme that provides leasable spaces to flight catering companies, banquet hall owners, and hospitals along with providing space to large chain restaurants to set up their main kitchen and serve all QSRs within a logical distance of the outlets (refer TAJ-SATS, Madras; Mish Horesha Kitchen Consultancy, other industry experts).

Dairy and Butchery—Due to the heavy demand of milk products and meat auxiliary, components such as dairy and butchery are required to manufacture daily products as per everyday demands (refer Mish Horesha Consultancy).

Food Processing Units—This component also supports the daily requirements of the kitchens but is majorly important to convert all the products produced in organic farming so that nothing is wasted and cheap quality products are procured. In a government scheme of mega food parks, the government also proposed similar components on a very large scale. But the model didn't catch people's attraction due to the lack of commercial components, distance from the city and so on, which are taken care of in the overall scheme (refer Mish Horesha Consultancy).

Staff Support—Due to the demand of huge numbers of highly skilled staff members, a lot of people from the nearby cities and towns are expected and due to the odd working hours of the industry, their accommodation, entertainment, and refreshment are of the utmost importance. Also, students and professionals are expected to visit the place for short-term research work or crash courses and hence residential facilities along with other refreshment amenities have been provided.

Recycling Plants—These plants are one of the most important components in the whole scheme, as a huge amount of organic waste is expected to be released at the end of each day, which needs to be properly converted into products such as manures to reduce the overall cost of farming. This is also a step toward achieving net zero standards.

Existing Cases of Different Components of the Module

DLF Cyber Hub, Gurugram

Figure 9.1 Aerial view of DLF Cyber Hub, Gurugram

Strategic Location

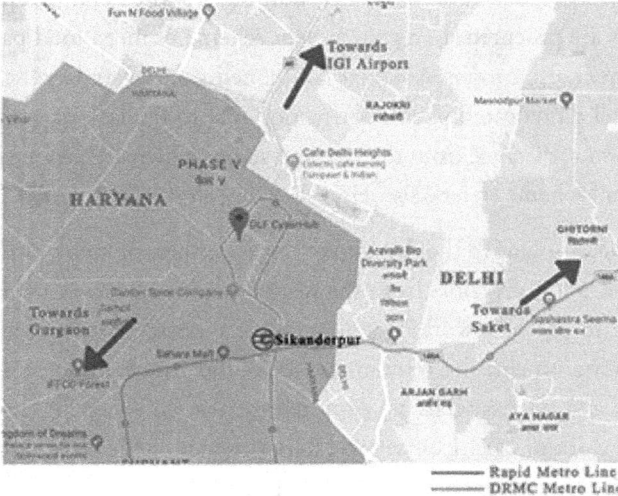

Figure 9.2 Location and accessibility of DLF Cyber Hub

Source: edited by author

This cyber hub is located in Gurugram, Haryana, on the periphery of the 3,000-acre DLF Cyber City. It is in close proximity to some important five-star business hotels like The Leela, Trident, and Oberoi. It is connected to the rest of the city through a 16-lane expressway on NH8. Also, it is well connected through Sikanderpur metro station (DMRC station) and IndusInd Bank Cyber City metro station (Rapid metro station), making it accessible from both South and Central Delhi.

Specific Information—The cyber hub is spread over a 200,000 ft.^{2} area and is surrounded by large MNC buildings. The total footfall at cyber hub is around 20,000 people each day.

Figure 9.3 *Master plan of DLF Cyber Hub*

Source: Gurugram, edited by author

DLF Cyber Hub is a privatized public space, located in the vicinity of DLF Cyber City, Gurugram. It is a very new concept in India as, despite being a large socializing zone, it has kept food at its core. It is situated in the heart of the Cyber City and offers unparalleled experiences to its users.

Figure 9.4 Plaza, DLF Cyber Hub

This uniquely designed plaza combines open and enclosed spaces and is visually influenced by its western counterparts. It has a really large open space for pedestrians and allows no vehicular movement inside the hub. The large walking spaces are filled with side cafes and eating joints on both the sides. There are shaded walkways which provide a smooth transition between the open and the built form, making the movement comfortable in all climatic conditions.

Figure 9.5 Shaded walkways, DLF Cyber Hub, Gurugram

The built form comprises three levels. Most of the restaurants present in these levels have kept open air seating as a major commercially productive option. Along with food outlets, a large amphitheatre and various other smaller congregation zones have been provided in order to increase public participation. These multi-functional spaces are large enough to hold a variety of public events from flash mobs, movie promotions, theater, and music concerts to large food festivals.

Figure 9.6 DLF Cyber Hub, Gurugram

Source: Author

A lot of thought has been employed in designing the street furniture, which helped in making the hub more attractive and comfortable for its users. Also, lighting has been a key point of focus for Cyber Hub as the place is more active during the evening.

Spaces like these increase the public comfort level and hence are becoming one of the best places to hang out today.

Analysis

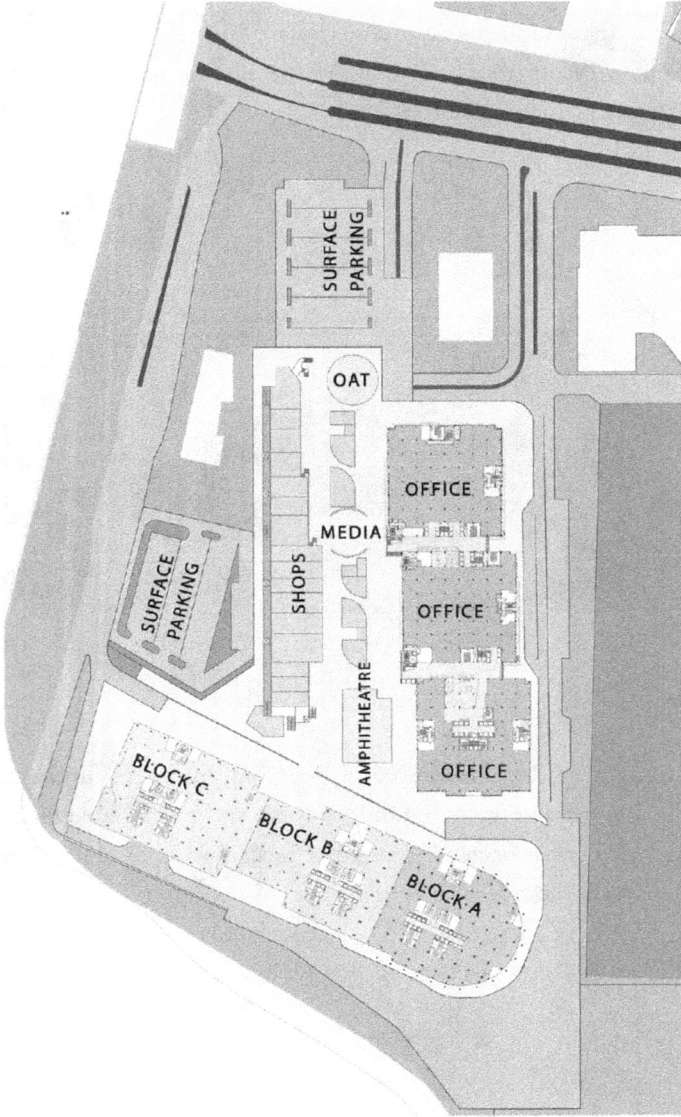

Figure 9.7 Site plan of DLF Cyber Hub, Gurugram

Source: edited by author

Precinct Study

Figure 9.8 Connectivity of DLF Cyber Hub, Gurgaon by road

Source: edited by author

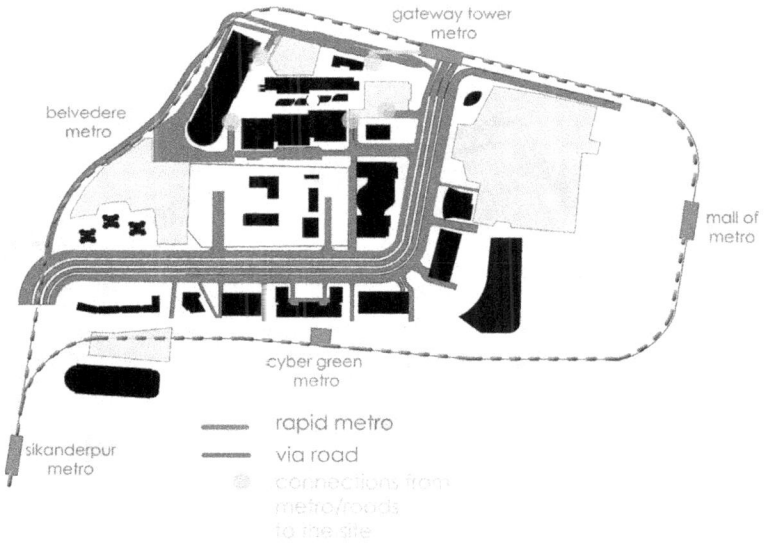

Figure 9.9 Metro connectivity of DLF Cyber Hub, Gurugram

Source: edited by author

Site Study

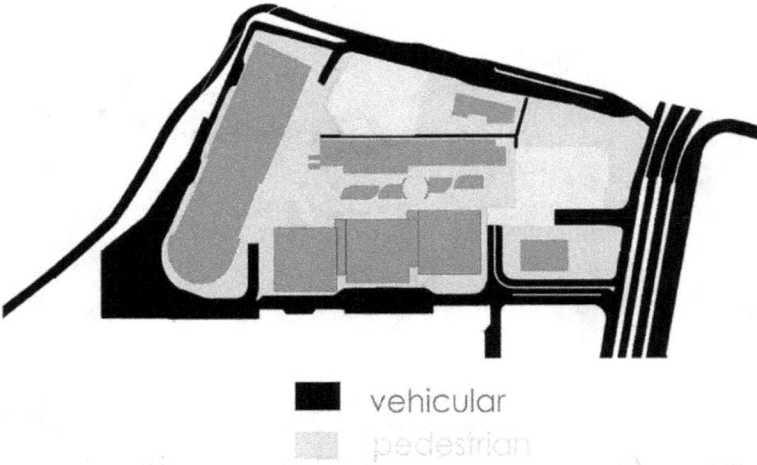

Figure 9.10 *Vehicular and pedestrian movement within DLF Cyber Hub*

Source: Author

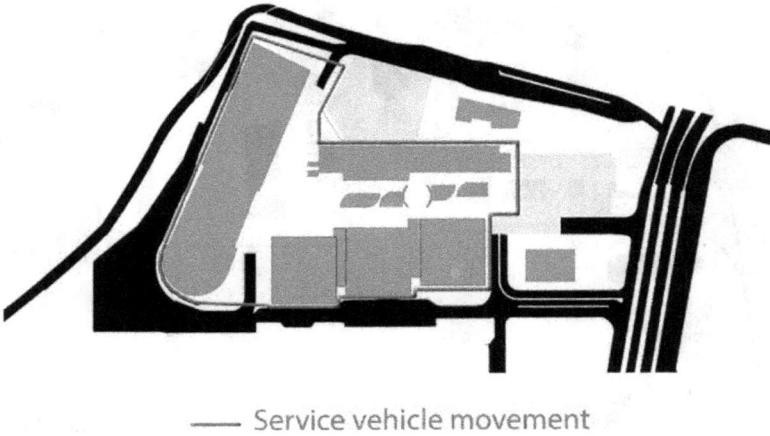

Figure 9.11 *Service vehicle movement, DLF Cyber Hub*

Source: Author

Functions

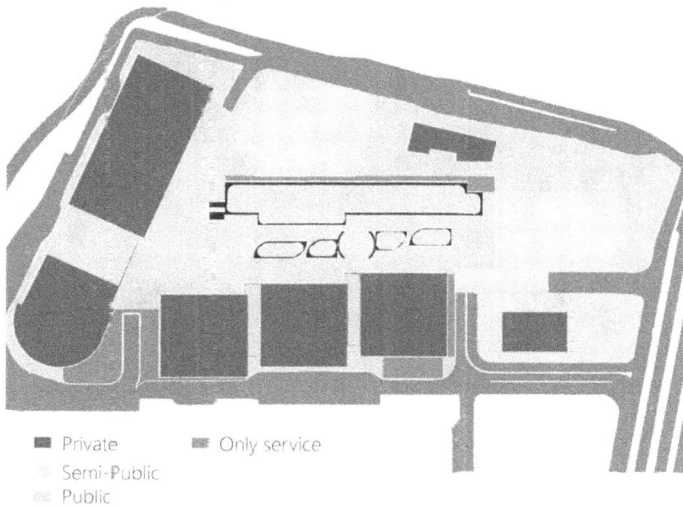

Figure 9.12 Hierarchy of functions, DLF Cyber Hub

Source: Author

Figure Ground Study

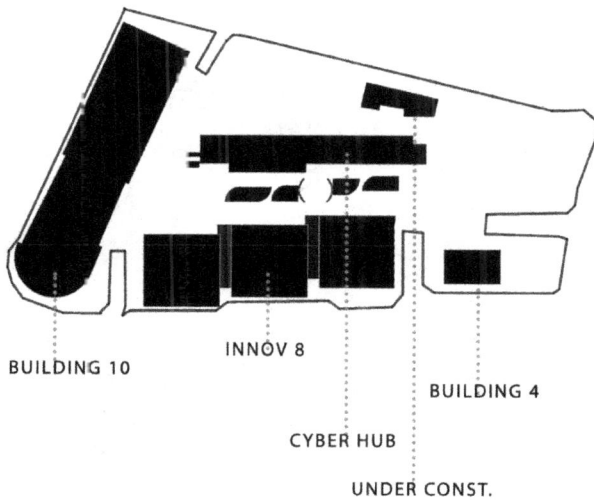

Figure 9.13 Figure ground: showing built-open relationship, DLF Cyber Hub

Source: Author

Figure 9.14 Back service corridor: (i) view from outside, covered with vertical greens, (ii) interior view of the corridor

A back-service entry corridor is covered with a jaali with vertical greens on it in order to hide it visually from the public. This green wall also acts as a buffer zone for the kitchens of different restaurants against the solar heat in an already heated area.

Figure 9.15 Jaali with vertical greens, DLF Cyber Hub, Gurugram

Olive Bistro and Bar, Cyber Hub, Gurugram

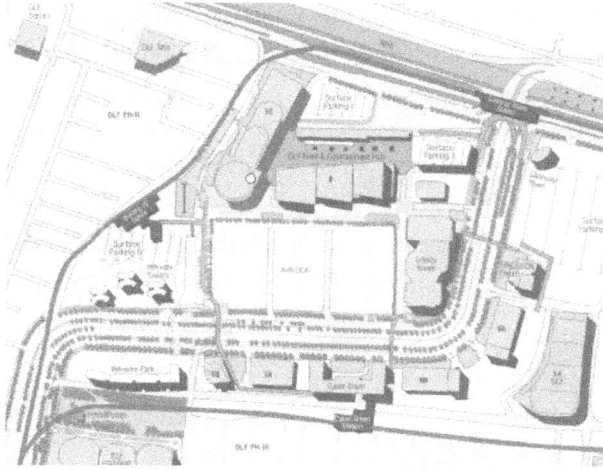

Figure 9.16 *Location of Olive Bistro and Bar in Cyber Hub, Gurugram*

Source: Author

Being at one of the major entrances of DLF Cyber Hub, Gurugram, the outlet of Olive Bistro and Bar has created quite a market for itself and is a restaurant that can cater to 125 people.

Through this case study, the back house mechanisms of restaurants were majorly studied.

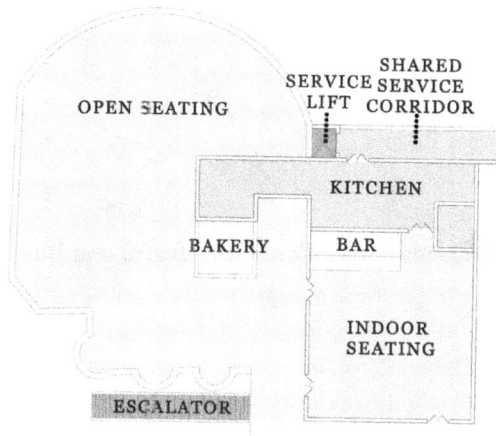

Figure 9.17 *Conceptual floor plan, Olive Bistro and Bar, edited by author*

Conceptual Floor Plan

Like this restaurant, all the restaurants are serviced from the common service corridor which has kitchen on one side and is protected and hidden with creepers from the other side.

Conceptual Roof Plan

The roof structure of this restaurant is specifically eye-catching as it is designed using tensile structures.

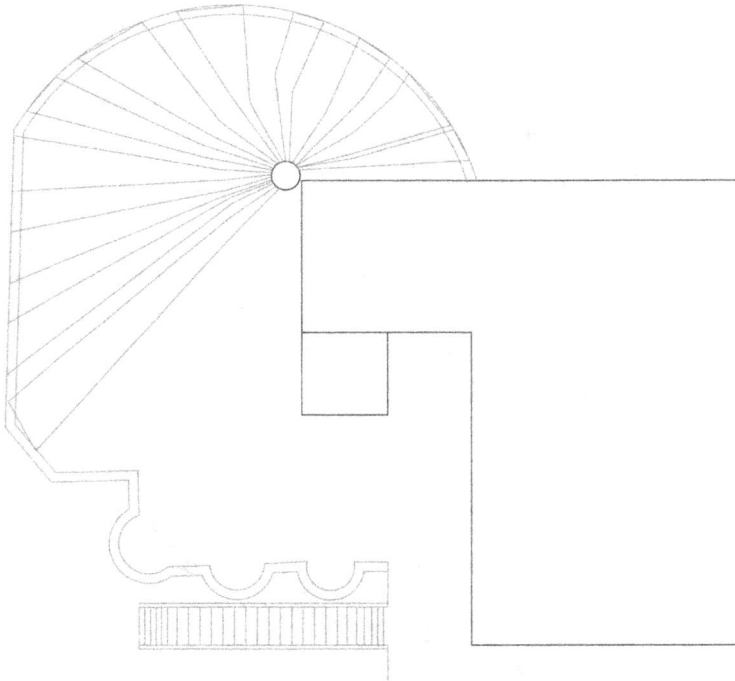

Figure 9.18 Conceptual roof plan, Olive Bistro and Bar

Analysis

Figure 19.19 Pictures of Olive Bistro and Bar, DLF Cyber Hub, Gurugram: (i) open seating area, (ii) interior view of the restaurant, (iii) kitchen area, and (iv) basement

A *large open seating area* has been provided with the best views of Cyber Hub. Along with open air seating, it also comprises an open bakery and semi-open tandoor section.

An *interior view of the indoor* seating of the restaurant shows seating for a total of 55 persons inside the restaurant, while the rest is in the open.

A *kitchen* with dimensions of 2 m × 7 m houses a team of 12 to 13 people who work for 12 to 14 h a day to cater to the restaurant, serving 175 to 200 people per hour.

The *basement* has a 2.5 m × 3 m large cold storage and deep freezer, which according to the head chef is enough for the given load.

Hotel Management Department, LPU, Jalandhar, Punjab

Figure 9.20 Building of Hotel Management Department, LPU, Jalandhar

Source: www.lpu.ac.in

Being one of the most renowned private universities of the country, the Lovely Professional University (LPU) provides the best infrastructure to its students from all fields. Hence the Hotel Management Department of the university, designed by Mr. Atul Singla (chief architect, LPU), is a case for study by architectural students to know the infrastructural needs of such an institution. According to the proposed project of the food park, the educational component, comprising the training, research, and exhibition facilities, needs to be appropriated from the space requirement that was assessed in the given case study. Also, the kinds of open spaces that were studied (not everything could be documented) were inspirational and gave a broad understanding of how the learning experience could be imbibed in the architectural space and hence produce a student-friendly built form.

While studying the detail of the spaces like the training kitchens, dummy kitchens, bakery, and laboratory, a rough estimate of area requirements for all equipment was assessed. This was very critical as these spaces are completely process driven and they must achieve full efficiency in all design as no compromise in this regard could be tolerated by the users. Since these spaces are majorly governed by large industrial equipment, aesthetical considerations come only after laying out initial schematic framework in the correct manner. Yet in this case, the architect successfully contributed in making interesting spaces for students, trainers, and faculties while keeping in mind the sustainability factors such as natural day lighting and natural ventilation in all its corridors, though the staff areas were a bit tight and could be opened up a little bit to make the offices liveable as well.

Figure 9.21 Hotel Management Department, LPU, Jalandhar

Source: www.lpu.ac.in

Floor Plan Analysis

The first three floors are used as a shopping mall whilst the upper floors of that portion are used as a hotel; hence, the drawings of the overall block were not provided. The part plans given in this chapter have been colour-coded to analyze different spaces according to the functions, occupants, and usability. It also shows the proportions of different areas.

Table 9.1 Area chart, Hotel Management Department, LPU, Jalandhar

SL	Function	Capacity (Sq. Ft.)	Area	Area/Person (Sq.Ft)	Sq.mt
1	Classroom A	55	576	10.5	0.97
2	Classroom B	75	1295	17.3	1.61
3	Classroom C	35	560	16	1.49
4	Laboratory	44	1085	24.7	2.29
5	Library	75	1140	15.2	1.41
6	Office	60	552	9.2	0.86
7	Kitchen	150	2684	17.9	1.66
8	Mess/Canteen	150	2800	18.7	1.74
9	Storeroom	20	420	21	1.95
10	Lobby	-	1280	-	-
11	Guest Room	2	220	110	10.23

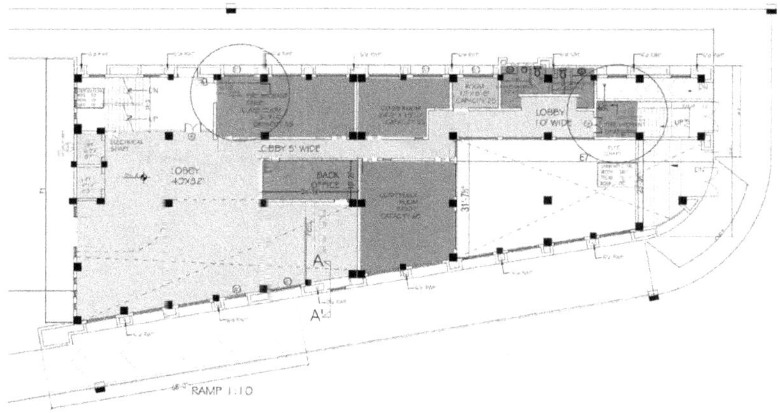

Figure 9.22 Ground floor part plan, LPU, Jalandhar, edited by author

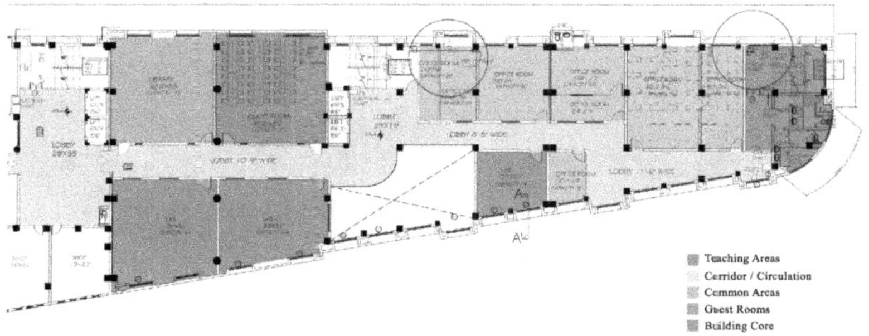

Figure 9.23 First floor part plan, LPU, Jalandhar, edited by author

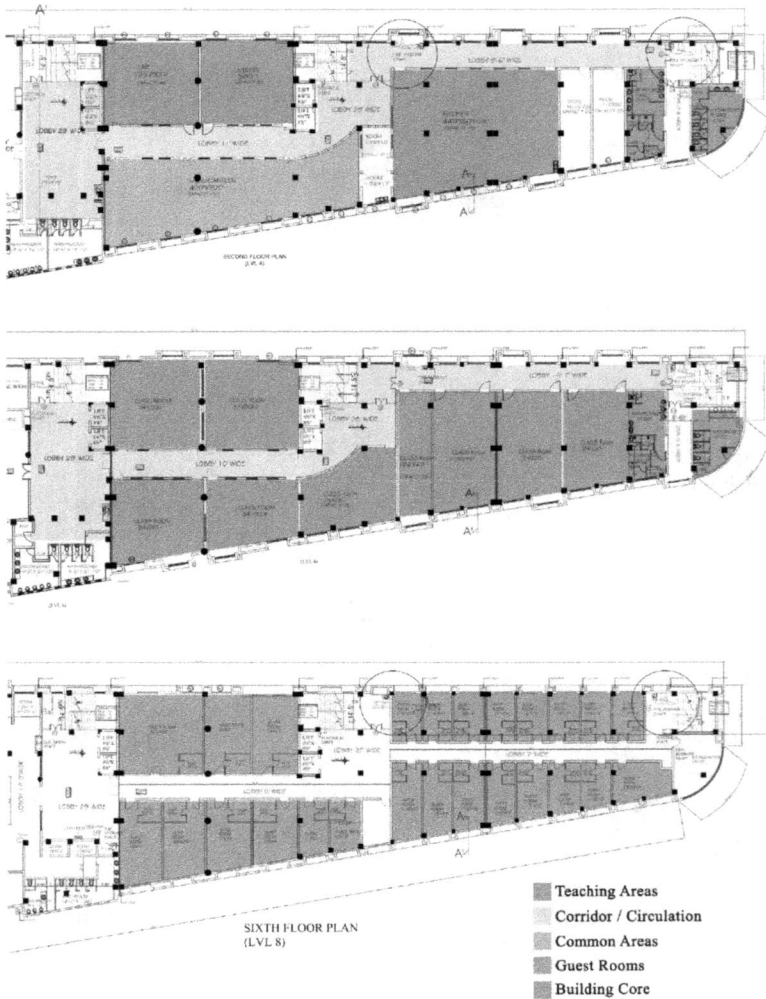

Figure 9.24 Part floor plans of the Hotel Management Department, LPU, Jalandhar: (i) second floor plan, (ii) third, fourth, and fifth floor plans and (iii) sixth floor plan, edited by author

Training Kitchen

Figure 9.25 Training kitchen, Hotel Management Department, LPU, Punjab

Source: Author

It is a typical training kitchen with a long array of gas burners and other working equipment required for a chef. It is important to understand the circulation as all the storage and equipment areas are on one side of the circulation space keeping the hot kitchen as a central island.

Figure 9.26 Kitchen equipment at the Hotel Management Department, LPU, Punjab

Source: Author

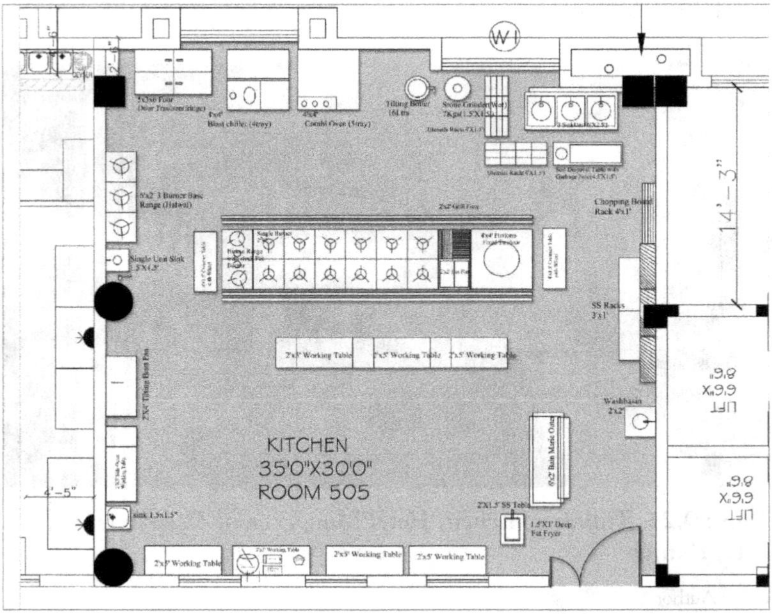

Figure 9.27 Training kitchen layout, Hotel Management Department, LPU, Punjab, edited by author

Figure 9.28 Training kitchen, Hotel Management Department, LPU, Jalandhar

Source: Author

Centre for Food Technology, University of Allahabad

Figure 9.29 Centre for Food Technology, University of Allahabad

The Centre for Food Technology, University of Allahabad, is a center of excellence dedicated to advanced research in the discipline of food technology. The new building is an extension of an old abandoned building which was rehabilitated and put to adaptive use as part of the center. As the center grew, the demand for more space facilitated design of the new state-of-the-art facilities, comprising dry and wet labs, research rooms, lecture and seminar rooms, library, and conferencing facilities. The building is located at a strategic location which marks the shift in orientation within the pedestrian network. This has a courtyard typology integrating the old building as a comprehensive whole, essentially a simplistic modern expression using glass and textured (Neev Architects Urban Designers Atelier n.d.). paint

Floor Plan Analysis

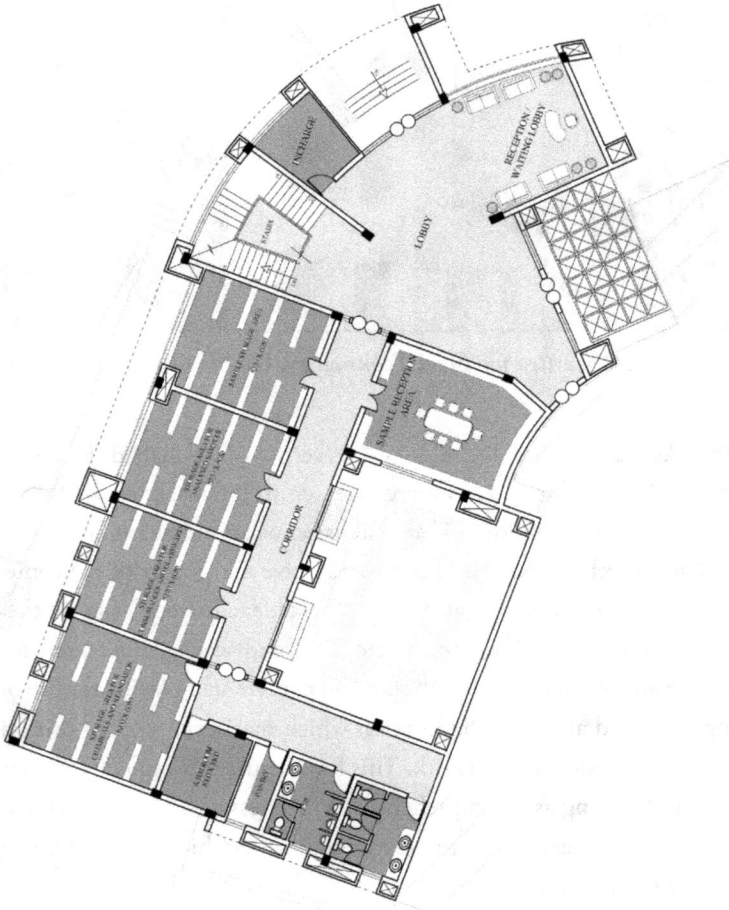

Figure 9.30 Ground floor plan, Centre for Food Technology, University of Allahabad, edited by author

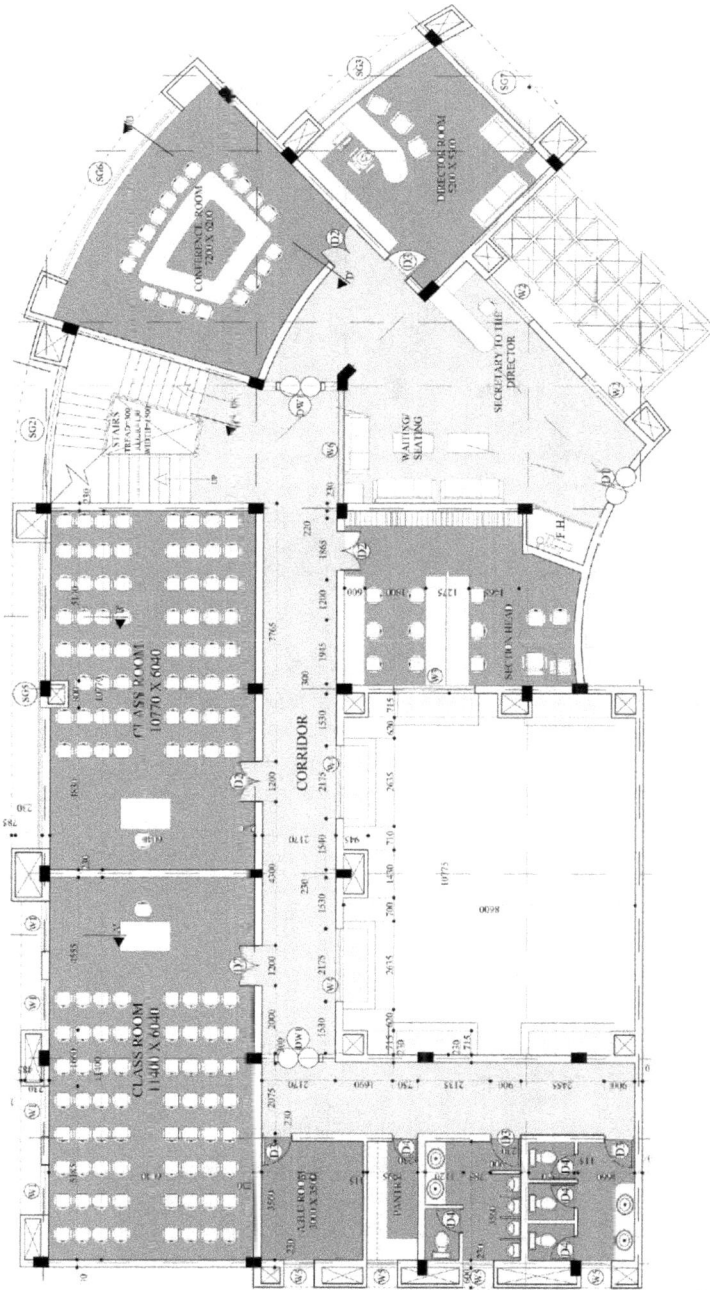

Figure 9.31 First floor plan, Centre for Food Technology, University of Allahabad, edited by author

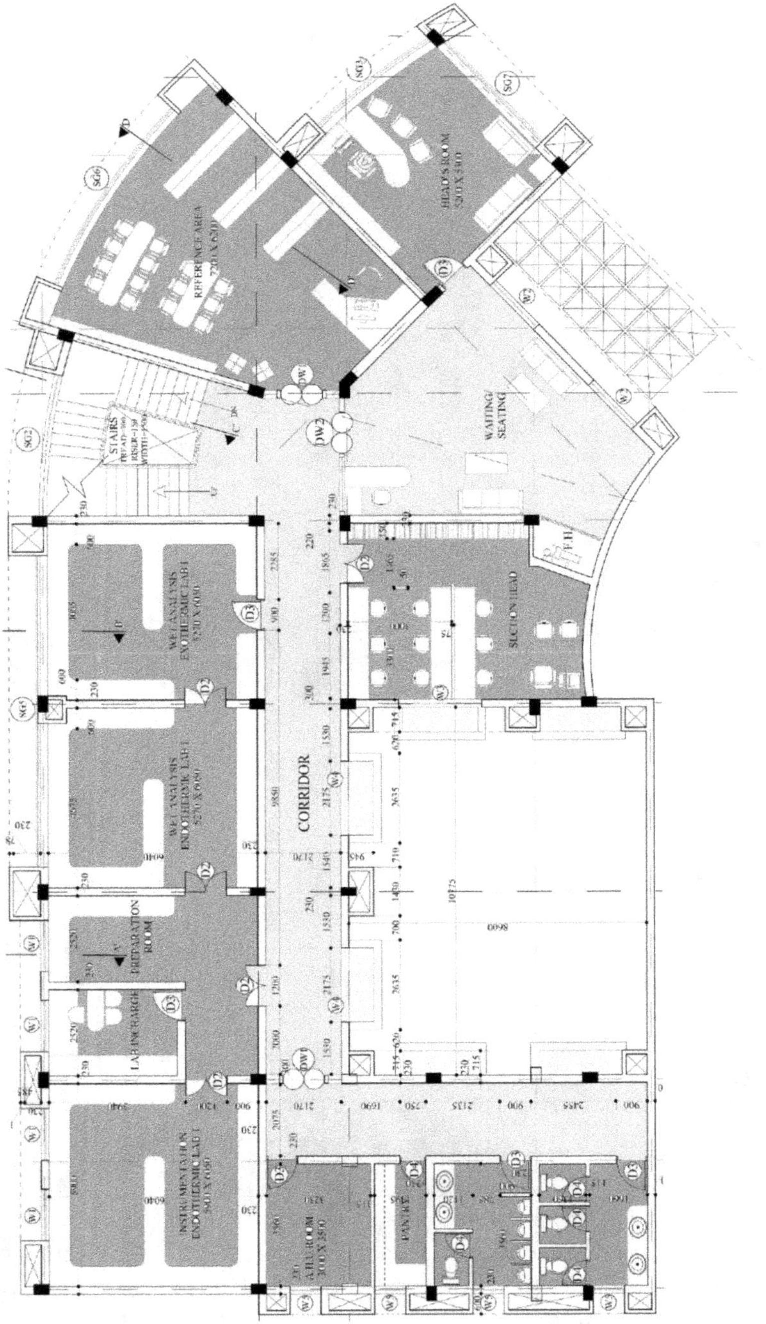

Figure 9.32 Third floor plan, Centre for Food Technology, University of Allahabad, edited by author

Area Chart

CENTRE FOR FOOD & TECHNOLOGY

AREA (GROUND FLOOR PLAN)	
SUB TOTAL (AREAS OF THE SHAFTS)	12.88
FLOOR PLATE AREA = 512.93-(AREAS OF THE SHAFTS) = 512.93-12.88 = **500.05 SqM**	

AREA (FIRST FLOOR PLAN)	
SUB TOTAL (AREAS OF THE SHAFTS)	12.86
FLOOR PLATE AREA = 528.74-(AREAS OF THE SHAFTS) = 528.74-12.86 = **515.88 SqM**	

AREA (SECOND FLOOR PLAN)	
SUB TOTAL (AREAS OF THE SHAFTS)	12.86
FLOOR PLATE AREA = 528.74-(AREAS OF THE SHAFTS) = 528.74-12.86 = **515.88 SqM**	

AREA (THIRD FLOOR PLAN)	
SUB TOTAL (AREAS OF THE SHAFTS)	12.86
FLOOR PLATE AREA = 528.74-(AREAS OF THE SHAFTS) = 528.74-12.86 = **515.88 SqM**	

TOTAL AREA	
GROUND FLOOR AREA	**505.05 SqM**
FIRST FLOOR AREA	**515.88 SqM**
SECOND FLOOR AREA	**515.88 SqM**
THIRD FLOOR AREA	**515.88 SqM**
TOTAL FLOOR AREA	**2052.69 SqM**

Figure 9.33 Area chart, Centre for Food Technology, University of Allahabad

Broad Area Programme

Table 9.2 Broad area programme, Centre for Food Technology, University of Allahabad

SL	Function	Capacity (Sq. Ft.)	Dimensions		Area	Area/ Person
			Length	Breadth	(SQ MT)	
1	Laboratories	25	7.95	6.05	48.1	1.92
2	Class room	64	11.4	6.05	68.97	1.08
3	Conference	25	7.2	6.2	44.64	1.79
4	Director room	1	5.2	5.3	27.56	27.56
5	Endothermic lab	25	5.9	6.05	35.7	1.43
6	Exothermic lab	25	5.27	6.05	31.88	1.28
7	Library	25	7.2	6.2	44.64	1.79
8	Incubation	25	5.27	6.05	31.88	1.28
9	Prep.room	5	2.6	5.9	15.34	3.07
10	Staff room	20	7.2	6.2	44.64	2.23

Source: Author

TAJ-SATS Flight Kitchen, Madras

Figure 9.34 Building of TAJ-SATS Flight Kitchen, Madras

Basic Statistics

Flights catered	120m^2
Meals prepared	11,000 m^2
Chefs	130 m^2
Staff	509 m^2
Recipes	1,200 m^2
Kitchen area	2,200 m^2

TAJ-SATS is a joint venture of TAJ Hotels and Resorts and SATS (Singapore Airport Terminal Services). It provides in-flight catering at Mumbai, Delhi, Chennai, Kolkata, and so on. It's a cross between a busy hotel kitchen and a sterile laboratory. Being the best in-flight catering company, the kitchen reflects a perfect blend between high-tech machinery and ultimate human skills.

The inside areas of such a functional space is depicted in Figure 9.35.

Figure 9.35 Interior views of the TAJ-SATS Flight Kitchen, Madras

Other Related Research and Findings

Basic Kitchen Layouts

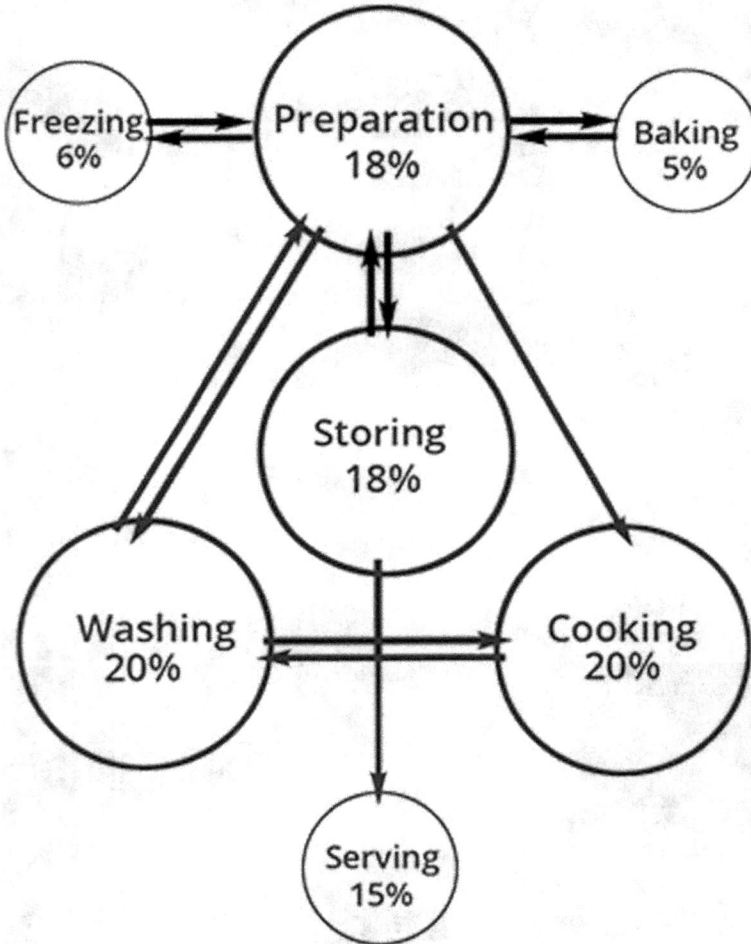

Figure 9.36 Schematic diagram of a kitchen

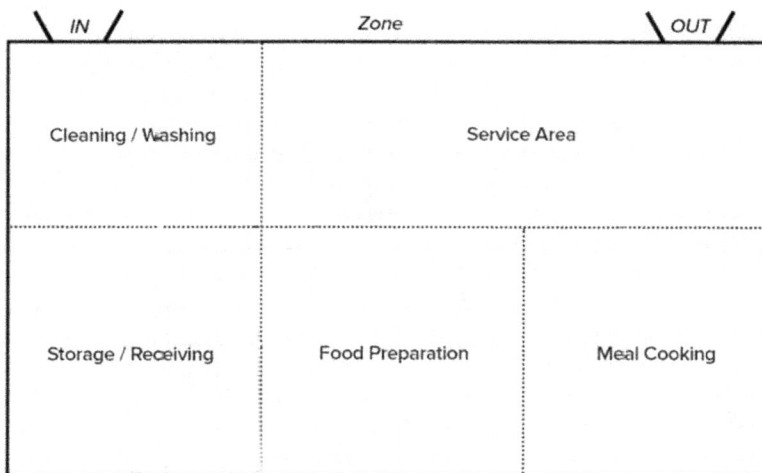

Figure 9.37 Typical zones in a kitchen

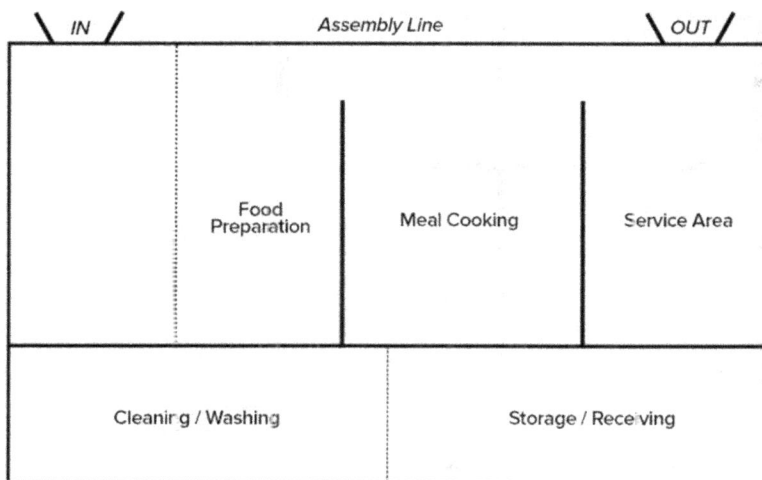

Figure 9.38 Typical zones in an assembly line kitchen

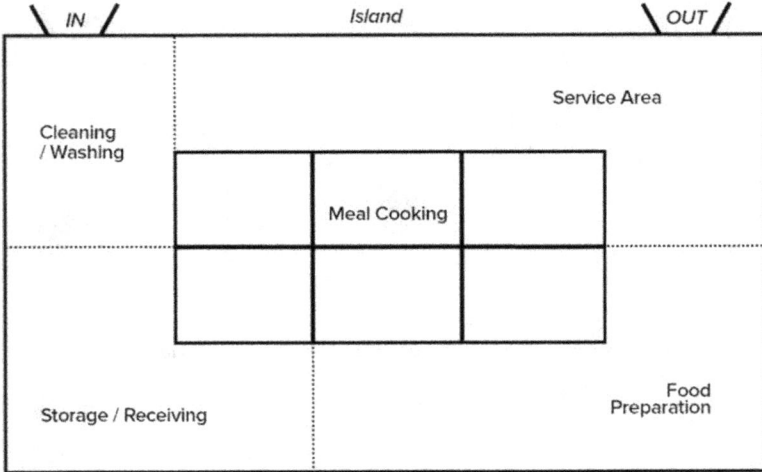

Figure 9.39 Typical island kitchen layout

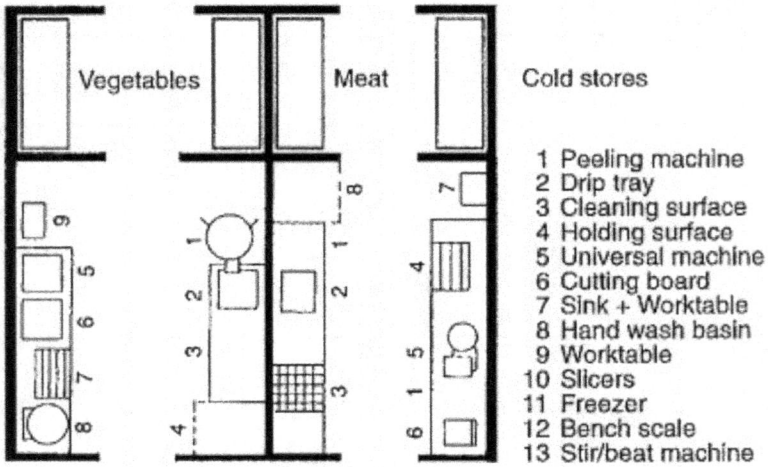

Figure 9.40 Separate preparation area for vegetables and meat

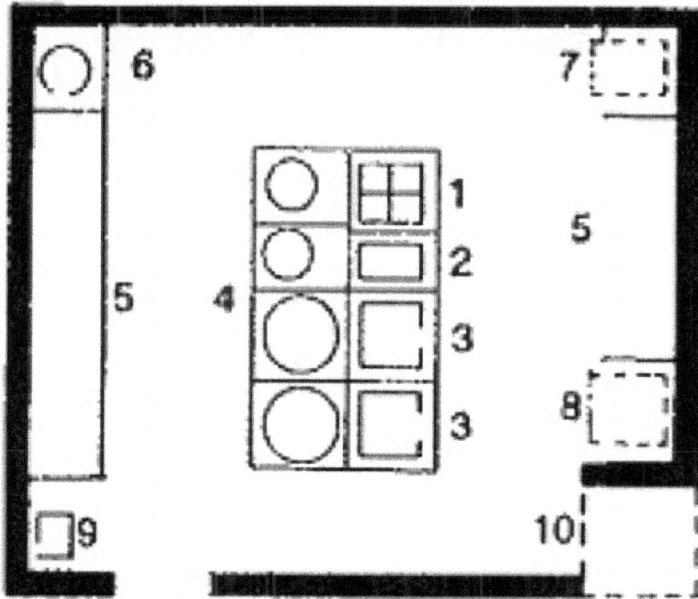

Figure 9.41 Hot kitchen layout

1 cooker
2 deep fat fryer
3 griddle
4 water boiler
5 work surface

6 cooker
7 double-deck oven
8 convectomat
9 hand basin
10 storage area

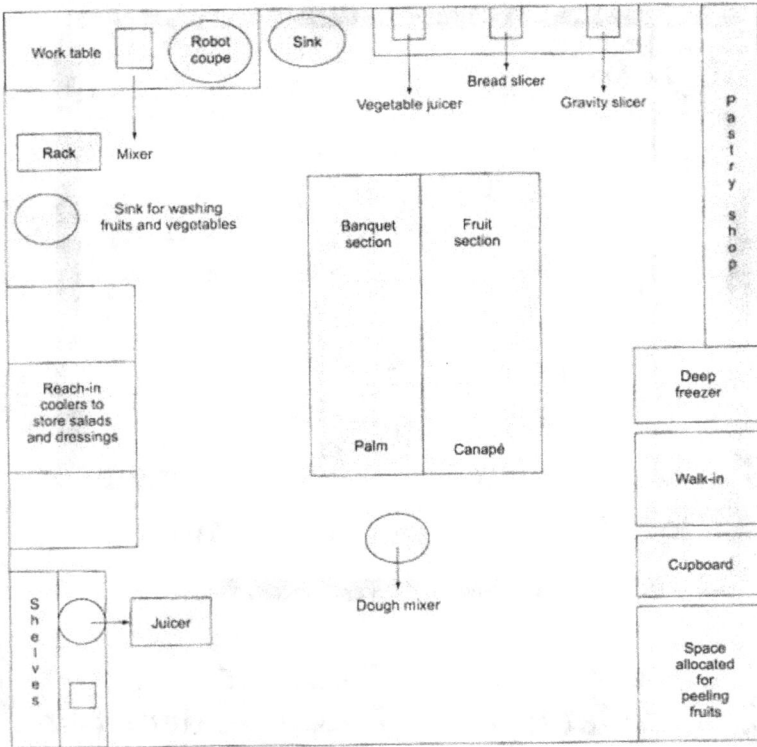

Figure 9.42 Cold kitchen layout

CHAPTER 10

Food Park: Background Research

Present Business Models—Studying the McDonald's Supply Chain

Currently, McDonald's India sources 90 percent of its products, raw food and semi-processed food through local vendors all over the country. Hence, there are a lot of hands involved in the overall process which increases the chance of recipe leak. The 10 percent outsourcing, which includes the secret recipe, therefore, can never be manufactured locally. The present model involves a lot of preservation cost as the semi-cooked materials need more care while transporting them, adding up to the overall cost.

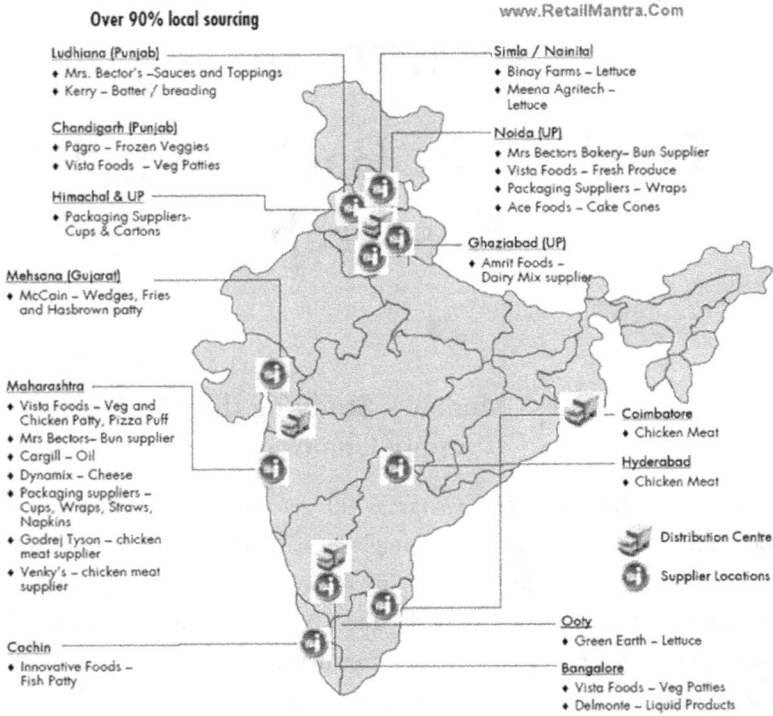

Figure 10.1 Map of India depicting 90 percent of the local sourcing of McDonald's

Source: www.retailmantra.com

Existing Supply Chain of McDonald's

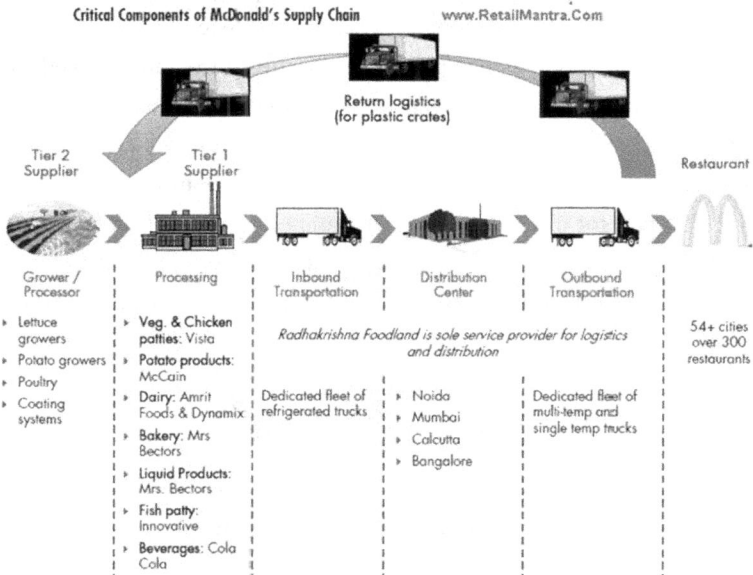

Figure 10.2 Critical components of McDonald's India supply chain

Source: www.retailmantra.com

Proposed Supply Chain for McDonald's

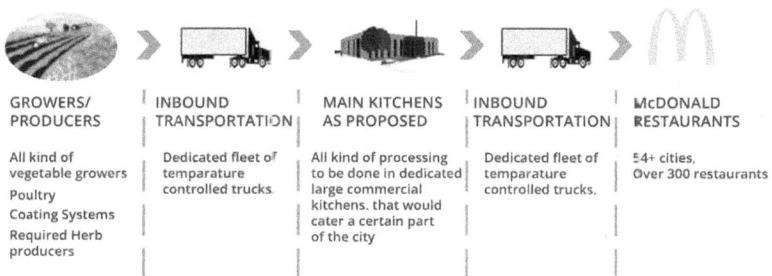

Figure 10.3 Proposed supply chain for McDonald's India

Source: Author

Although only one QSR brand has been studied, through experts in the field it has been cleared that most of the brands follow similar business models. So, in the proposed idea, the middlemen of the game, mostly the food producers and suppliers, are removed. Rather a more direct connection between the kitchen and the raw material producers is being created so that a large number of employees can be employed directly under the certain QSR brand and they process and produce the semi-cooked food directly in-house. Hence better quality control can be done. Recipes need not go to various hands. The large transportation cost will come down as more local producers will start tying up with such brands and will exclusively produce for them. Also, any harmful mixing or improper packaging of any ingredient will not affect the restaurants throughout the country. Rather a particular area will be affected, reducing the overall loss incurred by the company.

Context and Site Study

Influence Zone—Area that is the major target audience to the given food hubs based on scale, variety, accessibility, and so on.

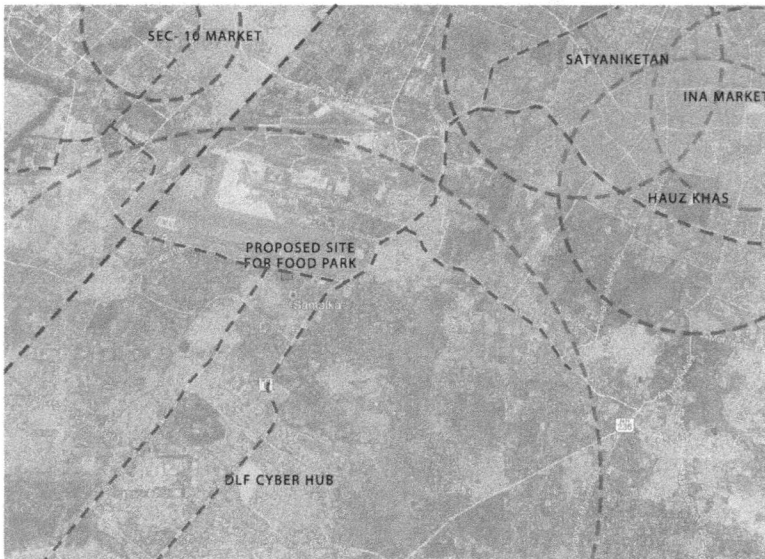

Figure 10.4 Influence zones around the site

Source: edited by author

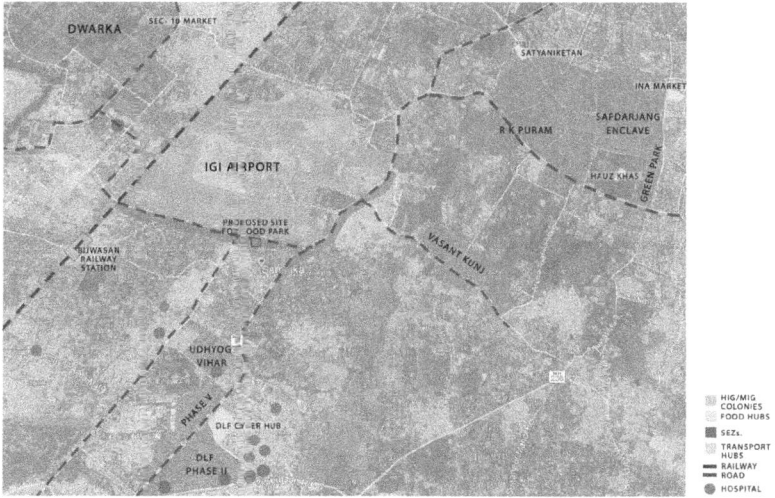

Figure 10.5 Context study

Source: edited by author

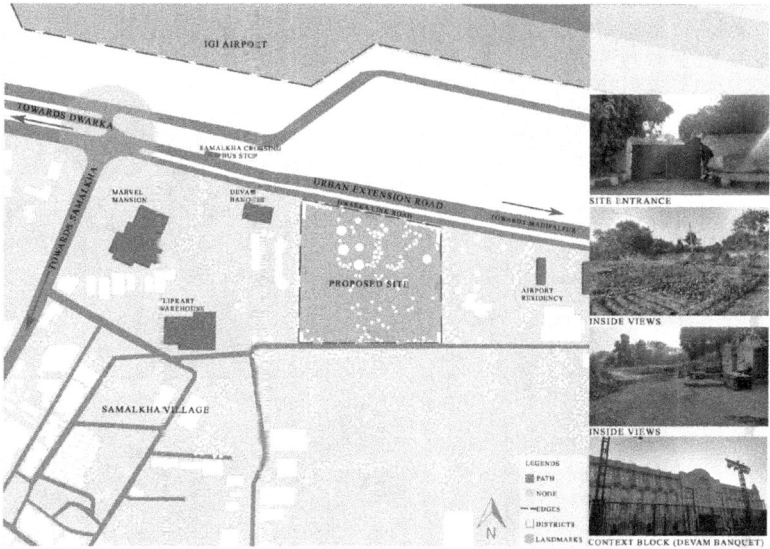

Figure 10.6 Context and site study, Samalkha, Delhi

Source: Author

Climatic Study of the Site

At Indira Gandhi International Airport, the wet season is sweltering, oppressive, and partly cloudy and the dry season is warm and mostly clear. Over the course of the year, the temperature typically varies from 5°C to 45°C. The clearer part of the year at Indira Gandhi International Airport begins around September 3 and lasts for 10 months, ending around July 5. On October 14, the clearest day of the year, the sky is clear, mostly clear or partly cloudy 96 percent of the time, and overcast or mostly cloudy 4 percent of the time.

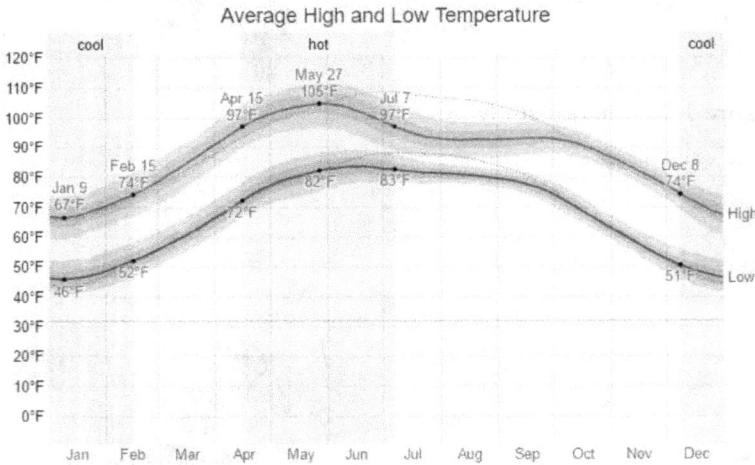

Figure 10.7 Average temperature chart of the site at Samalkha, Delhi, in Fahrenheit

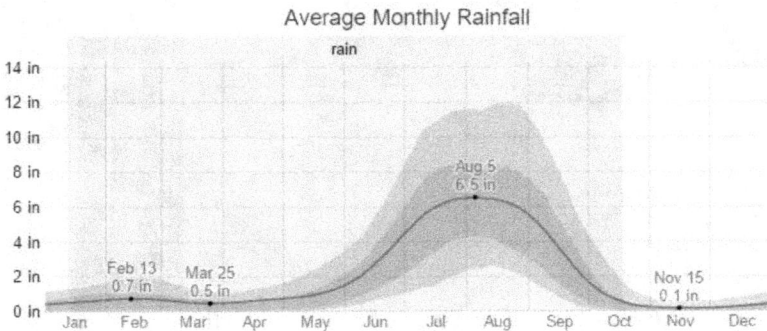

Figure 10.8 Average monthly rainfall in inches

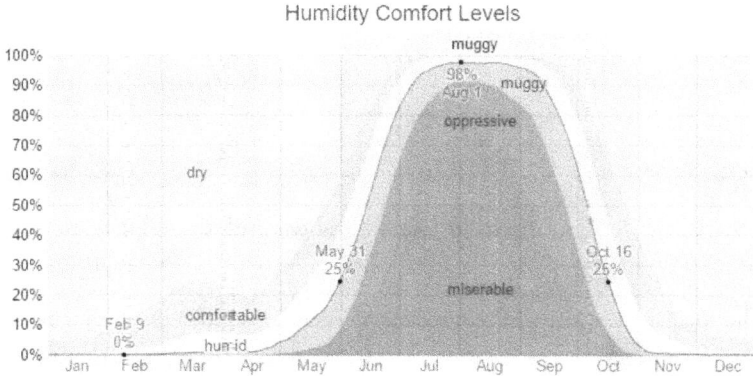

Figure 10.9 Humidity comfort level

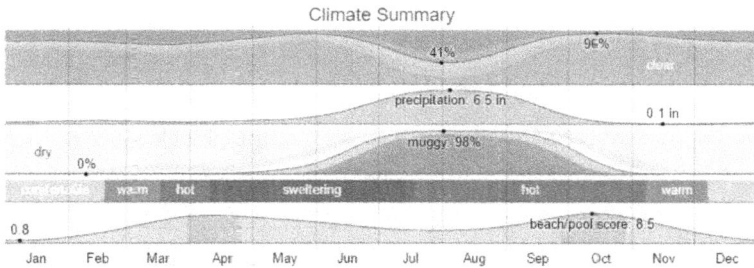

Figure 10.10 Climate summary of Samalkha, Delhi

The wetter season lasts for 3.0 months, from June 15 to September 14, with a greater than 27 percent chance of a given day being a wet day. The humidity comfort level depends on the dew point, as it determines whether perspiration will evaporate from the skin, thereby cooling the body. Lower dew points feel drier and higher dew points feel more humid. The muggier period of the year lasts for 4.5 months, from May 31 to October 16, during which time the comfort level is muggy, oppressive, or miserable.

Month of year		Jan	Feb	Mar	Apr	May	Jun	Jul	Aug	Sep	Oct	Nov	Dec	Year
		01	02	03	04	05	06	07	08	09	10	11	12	1-12
Dominant wind direction		▲	▲	▲	▲	▲	▲	▼	▼	▲	◄	▲	►	▲
Wind probability >= 4 Beaufort (%)		4	7	9	10	10	13	6	5	6	3	2	3	8
Average Wind speed (kts)														
		6	7	7	8	8	8	7	7	7	6	6	6	6
Average air temp (°C)		16	21	27	34	37	36	32	32	32	30	24	19	28

Figure 10.11 Wind speed in "knot" and dominant wind direction

The local wind flow direction is north-west to south-east with a reverse flow in monsoon season variation. The average wind speed varies from 4 to 13 knots with the windier months from February to July.

Area Programme

The area programme consists of the following functions—main kitchen, dairy, butchery, food processing unit, food court, research and training center, an agro-based mall, staff support, admin block, and recycling plants area. The area allocated for each function is specified in.

	TOTAL AREA REQUIREMENTS		
SL.NO	NAME	AREA	AREA (SQ MT)
1	FOODCOURT	85890	7988
2	RESEARCH AND TRAINING CENTRE	32704	3041
3	AGRO-BASED MALL	48160	4479
4	MAIN KITCHEN	41300	3841
5	DAIRY	1890	176
6	BUTCHERY	1414	132
7	FOOD PROCESSING UNIT	2660	247
8	STAFF SUPPORT	28350	2637
9	RECYCLING PLANTS	4000	372
10	GENERAL SERVICING	12320	1146
11	ADMIN	4158	387
	TOTAL	262846	24445

Figure 10.12 Area programme for the food park at Samalkha, Delhi

Source: Author

Area Programme

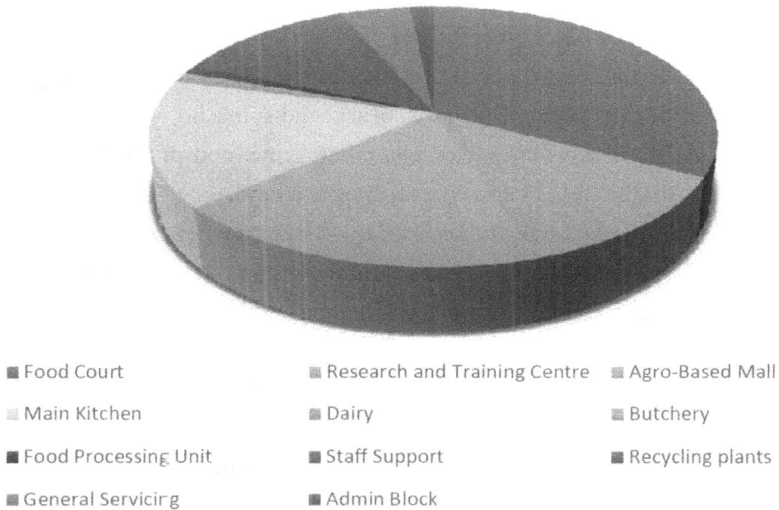

■ Food Court   ▨ Research and Training Centre   ▨ Agro-Based Mall

▨ Main Kitchen   ▨ Dairy   ▨ Butchery

■ Food Processing Unit   ■ Staff Support   ■ Recycling plants

■ General Servicing   ■ Admin Block

Figure 10.13 Pie chart depicting the areas allocated to each function

Source: Author

Technology

Passive Strategies toward Sustainability

Location of Water Bodies—Water is a good modifier of micro-climate. It takes up large amount of heat in evaporation and causes significant cooling. Water has a moderating effect on the air temperature of the micro-climate. It possesses very high thermal storage capacity, much higher than building materials like brick, concrete, and stone. Large bodies of water in the form of lake, river, and fountain generally have a moderating effect on the temperature of the surrounding area due to the higher thermal storage capacity of water compared to land and cause variations in airflow. During the day the air is hotter over the land and rises, drawing cooler air in from the water mass resulting in land breezes. During the night as the land mass cools quicker, the airflow will be reversed. Water evaporation has a cooling effect on the surroundings.

Façade Treatment

- *Vertical Gardening/Green Wall*
  i. Trellis or vertical framing for creepers. One can grow food-producing creepers like peas, beans, and spinach.
  ii. Modular walls, potted plants can grow food-producing plants and herbs like lettuce, oregano, and basil.
- *Green Buffer through Landscaping*—Trees grown on edges of the built form to provide natural shading to the surfaces exposed to sun. Trees such as Champa and Mulberry are preferable for this purpose.
- *Vertical Louvers*—Extremely useful to cut the direct sun light.
- *Double Wall*—Double-wall construction is considered to be "above grade" or, in other words, a premium wall design because
  i.   It provides more structural integrity and has exceptional energy performance.
  ii. Of its less electricity and heat usage.
  iii. Overtime, this can save a lot of money due to growing energy costs.
  iv. It provides an excellent air/vapor barrier support and noise reduction.

- *Use of Fly-Ash Blocks*
  i.   It is a light-weight material compared to clay bricks, so it is suitable for multi-storey buildings.
  ii. It absorbs less amount of heat.
  iii. Uniform shape—hence no plastering required if used for compound wall or godowns.
  iv. Less mortar required in construction, because all bricks are machine made and even in shape.
  v.   High compressive strength as compared to normal bricks—no more wastages during transport.
  vi. It is less porous and absorbs very little water, whereas burnt clay bricks absorb more water during construction.

- *DGU Glass*
    i. It is very good for heat insulation
    ii. It provides very good sound insulation in between the interiors and exteriors.
    iii. It is resistant to UV light and prevents the fading of fabric and furniture.
    iv. Tempered glass, heat-strengthened glass could also be used, making it a safety glass.

Green Roof

- Green roof provides 25 percent additional insulation to the building.
- It helps in absorbing sound.
- Improves the quality of air and enhances the air movement.
- It provides a space to grow kitchen garden/organic garden.

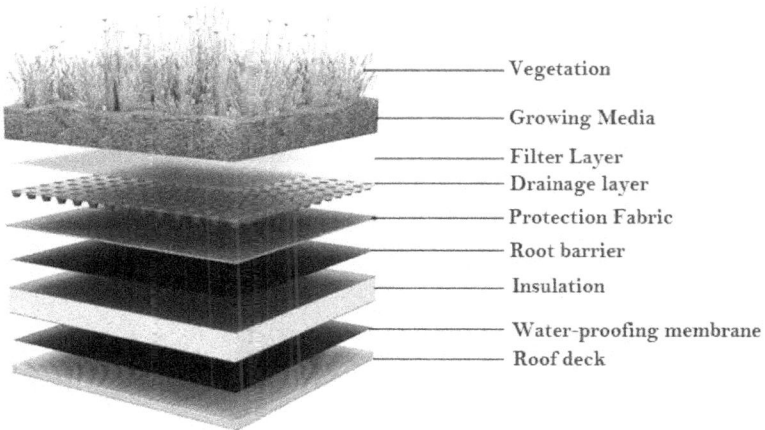

Vegetation
Growing Media
Filter Layer
Drainage layer
Protection Fabric
Root barrier
Insulation
Water-proofing membrane
Roof deck

Figure 10.14 Components of a green roof

Source: www.greenmylife.com

CHAPTER 11

Conceptual Design for a Food Hub Module at Samalkha, New Delhi

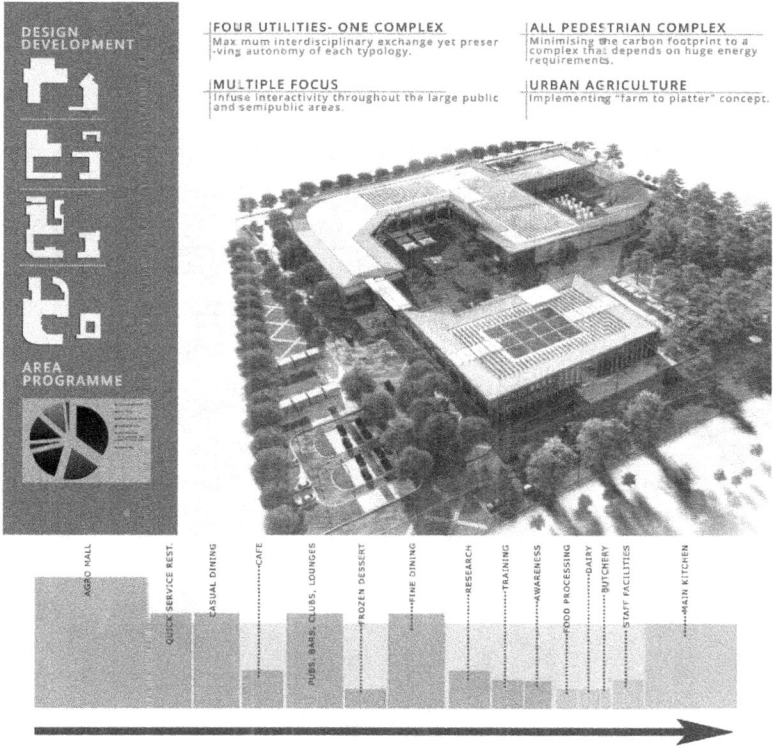

Figure 11.1 Concept design for a food hub module at Samalkha, New Delhi

Source: Author

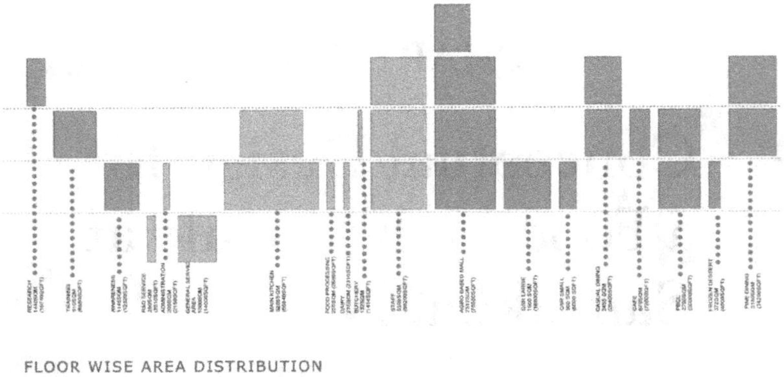

FLOOR WISE AREA DISTRIBUTION

Figure 11.2 Floor-wise area distribution chart

Source: Author

Linear Organization

An integrated complex was proposed that allows the public to flow through the commercial complex, witnessing the research components and the exhibition areas rather than restricting them in the periphery of the built mass. Programs are organized as a public street leading toward the focus-built forms. The linear formation gives all the visitors a full view of all the activities happening rather than strongly dividing into back of the house and front of the house.

Site Plan—Food Hub Module, Samalkha, New Delhi

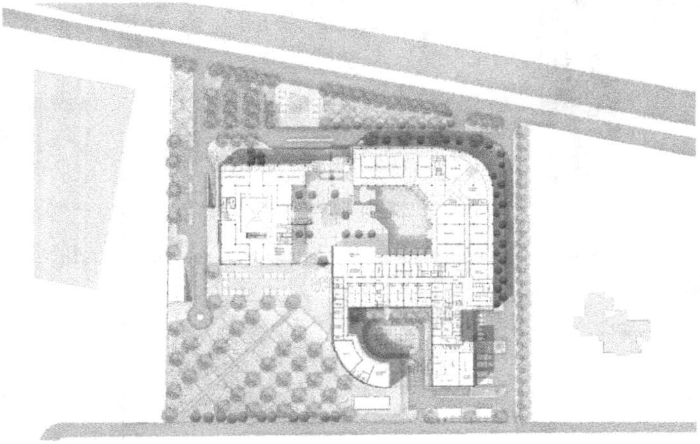

Figure 11.3 Site plan for a food hub module, Samalkha, New Delhi

Figure 11.4 3D visualization of food hub module, Samalkha, New Delhi

Source: Author

Figure 11.5 3D visualization of food hub module, Samalkha, New Delhi

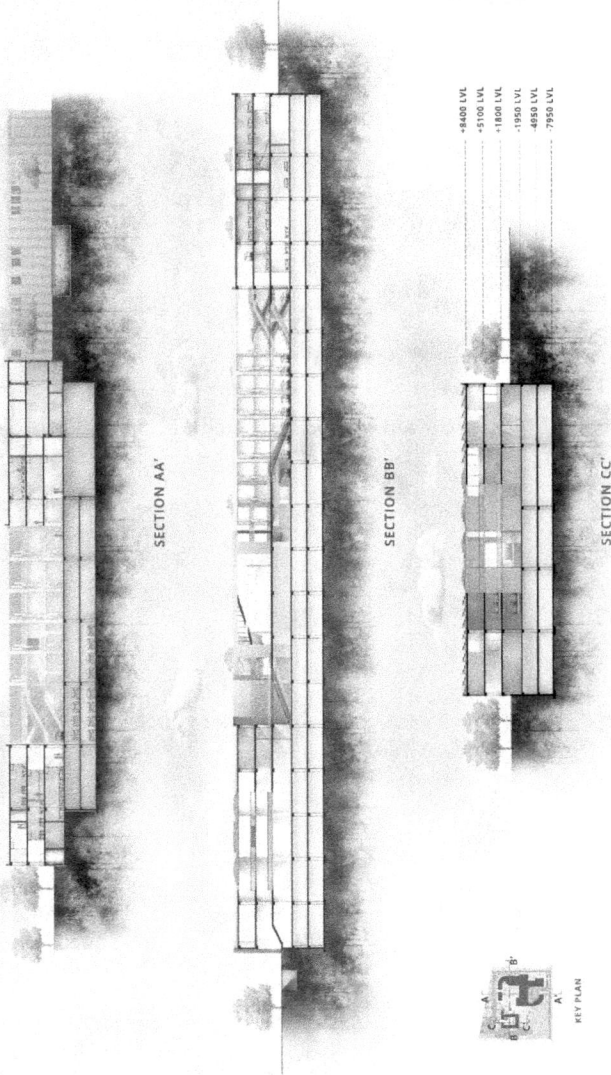

Figure 11.6 Architectural sections, food hub module, Samalkha, New Delhi

Source: Author

Figure 11.7 3D views of the complex

Source: Author

Bibliography

Andreini, L. 2000. *Cafés and Restaurants*. Milan: teNeues Media GmbH & Co. KG.

Armrest, F.F. 2003. *Near a Thousand Tables: A History of Food*. Free Press.

Beck, G. 1995. *Form in the Era of Fun*.

Benjamin, W. 1936. *The Work of Art in the Age of Mechanical Reproduction*. Schocken/Random House, ed. by Hannah Arendt.

Das, S. 2002. *Theme Based Restaurant. Dissertation*. New Delhi, India: School of Planning and Architecture, New Delhi.

Gao. 2012. *100 Restaurant Design principles*.

Ginal. February 28, 2003. *Summary: The Work of Art in The Age of Mechanical Reproduction*. Retrieved from Introducing the Frankfurt School: https://frankfurtschool.wordpress.com/2008/02/28/summary-the-work-of-art-in-the-age-of-mechanical-reproduction/

Hall, C.M., and S. Gössling. 2016. *Food Tourism and Regional Development: Networks, Products and Trajectories* (Routledge Studies of Gastronomy, Food and Drink), ed. Routledge.

ITC Hotels. (n.d.). Retrieved from ITC Hotels: http://itchotels.in/bukhara

Kunz, M.N., and J. Fischer. 2005. *Café & Restaurant Design*. teNeues.

Lefebvre, H. 1992. *The Production of Space*.

Neev Architects Urban Designers Atelier. (n.d.). Retrieved from NAUDA: http://nauda.co/project/arch/architectureinst-foodtech.html

Oldenburg, R. 1999. *The Great Good Place: Cafes, Coffee Shops, Bookstores, Bars, Hair Salons, and Other Hangouts at the Heart of a Community*, 3 ed. Da Capo Press.

Parham, S. 2015. *Food and Urbanism*. Bloomsbury.

Restaurant Design Guidelines, The City of Scottsdale. 2000.

Rockwell, D. (n.d.). (M. Kaplan, Interviewer)

Russell, J. 1997. *Entertainment Retail: Theming vs. Design*.

Scafidi, S. 2005. *Who Owns Culture?: Appropriation and Authenticity in American Law Public Life of the Arts Series Rutgers series on the public life of the arts*. Rutgers University Press.

Schultz, D. 2000. *Restaurant Aesthetics*.

Simpson, R. 2003. *Theme and Experience in Restaurant Design*.

Thorpe, A. 2012. *Architecture & Design versus Consumerism: How Design Activism Confronts Growth*. Routledge; 1 edition.

About the Authors

Prof. (Chef) Subhadip Majumder, Masters in Hotel Management and Certified Hospitality Educator of AHLEI, is a seasoned hospitality academician, culinary professional, researcher, author, and spiritual and humanity contributor to the society having numerous achievements under his name. He has been recognized as a visionary with extensive expertise in food production and quality control in culinary fields along with the preparation of SOPs and its implementation, profit generation, skill development, talent sharing, module and curriculum development, architectural guidance, placement assistance, and business module development.

This multifaceted personality with galore of global experience has won many prestigious awards like "The Preficio Award 2020 for best Humanity Service as Hospitality Professional," "Best Hospitality Guru—2019," "Culinary Educator Award—2018," "Performance Excellent Award by REAA 2018" and "Professional Excellence Award for Lifetime Achievement" by Sri Sathya Sai Seva Organisation India. He is working as freelancer and apart from his mentioned skills, he is working on the architectural development of organizations in relation to gastronomy.

Ar. Sounak Majumder, B Arch, School of Planning and Architecture, New Delhi, is the co-founder of Delhi-based architectural firm "Design Cult." He is also the co-founder of Reroute, a platform to promote alternate architectural education to the students and young architects of the country. He has also worked as a graduate architect at Systra India Limited and worked on urban-scale metro projects in India and abroad. Currently he is working on varied large- and small-scale architectural and landscape projects, while handling logistics and social media for Reroute. Being a food enthusiast, he has authored several journals and papers.

Index

Veranda, 33
Vertical gardening/green wall, 98
Vertical louvers, 98
Visual imagery, 43–44

Water bodies, 97

Work of Art in the Age of Mechanical
    Reproduction, The
    (Benjamin), 19
Wright, F. L., 3

Zamindar's veranda, 33

OTHER TITLES IN THE TOURISM AND HOSPITALITY MANAGEMENT COLLECTION

Betsy Bender Stringam, New Mexico State University, Editor

- *Cultural and Heritage Tourism and Management* by Tammie J. Kaufman
- *Marine Tourism, Climate Change, and Resilience in the Caribbean, Volume II* by Kreg Ettenger and Samantha Hogenson
- *Marketing Essentials for Independent Lodging* by Pamela Lanier and Marie Lanier
- *Marine Tourism, Climate Change, and Resiliency in the Caribbean, Volume I* by Kreg Ettenger and Samantha Hogenson
- *Catering and Convention Service Survival Guide in Hotels and Casinos* by Lisa Lynn Backus and Patti J. Shock
- *Coastal Tourism, Sustainability, and Climate Change in the Caribbean, Volume II* by Martha Honey and Kreg Ettenger
- *Coastal Tourism, Sustainability, and Climate Change in the Caribbean, Volume I* by Martha Honey and Kreg Ettenger
- *The Good Company* by Robert Girling and Heather Gordy

Concise and Applied Business Books

The Collection listed above is one of 30 business subject collections that Business Expert Press has grown to make BEP a premiere publisher of print and digital books. Our concise and applied books are for...

- Professionals and Practitioners
- Faculty who adopt our books for courses
- Librarians who know that BEP's Digital Libraries are a unique way to offer students ebooks to download, not restricted with any digital rights management
- Executive Training Course Leaders
- Business Seminar Organizers

Business Expert Press books are for anyone who needs to dig deeper on business ideas, goals, and solutions to everyday problems. Whether one print book, one ebook, or buying a digital library of 110 ebooks, we remain the affordable and smart way to be business smart. For more information, please visit www.businessexpertpress.com, or contact sales@businessexpertpress.com.

www.ingramcontent.com/pod-product-compliance
Lightning Source LLC
Chambersburg PA
CBHW061334220326
41599CB00026B/5190